CROP CIRCLE

MESSAGES

FROM THE

STARS

Awakening to Multi-Dimensional
Consciousness

Published by STAR TEMPLE PRESS

www.PleiadianRegression.co.uk

www.AmumaRa.com

ISBN: 978-0-9926213-0-8

STAR CONNECTING

... We have called you to do this work to help people learn to connect to their star beings, and thus to all star beings. For once a soul is awake in their star being, and has cleared their channels, they can communicate with all star beings and angelic beings, for they are able to exist on many planes at once: they have become multi-dimensional beings.

Metatron, 14 September 2012

CONTENTS

PREFACE

The Ascension Processes in our Times

The Master Hilarion:

Soon we enter the turbulent times, the times when many will seek for signs in the skies of the ending of your world. When this does not happen in the way many have been led to believe and they are not whisked away to a place of bliss in the Fifth Dimension, then confusion and despair will set in amongst very many of the souls who have been led astray. These souls have taken into their hearts the false thought - clinging to the hope of radical change which will come upon them, without their doing anything - that the world as they know it will end at the end of 2012. This thought has been planted by the dark forces to prevent the real possibility of ascension in these souls.

For ascension has always been possible for human beings who devote themselves to the spirit. It takes place as inner experience, as inner development, which lifts you up into true spirit experience. When you transform yourselves inwardly through your dedication to your spiritual path, then you prepare the seed-bed for us to work within you to effect the re-connection of your codes with that which it is possible in these times to develop. Working together in this way, you co-create with us, a new alignment and restructuring of your physical and etheric bodies.

First however it is necessary to purify your astral body – and this means your starry vehicle, dear ones. Working to clear the emotional blocks and confusions which result from earthly karma is one of the steps on this path. Establishing a daily rhythm of meditative practice is another step which will allows you to link consciously to spirit beings and star beings when you have gone far enough along the path. We will then be able to grant you great assistance as you ask us to work with you. As your starry body is refined it becomes transparent to us, and we to you, and you regain your connection to the stars. This is a process which takes dedicated work, dear ones, but it is a safe and sure path which will yield results.

There are quick ways, e.g. shortcuts through drugs, which promise to open your consciousness to spiritual life. And they do work, dear ones, as many of you know from experience, but when the foundation of solid meditative practice and cleansing of the astral vehicle – the emotional body - are not there, then you find you falter at the first trials that life throws at you and fall back to where you started from. Without your devoted daily spiritual practice and the cleansing of your emotional body, no path will lead you successfully to the desired goal of becoming a free and independent human being who is capable of consciously working alongside the star beings and spiritual masters.

You will be able to discern who has followed the long sure path by their ability to maintain their equilibrium through all the trials they pass through. This is the aim, to be able to stay steady and balanced and be able to act rightly in all situations of life. With such highly developed human souls we are glad to work, and will receive them into our ranks with joy and gratitude.

Dear souls, when you tread this path with true inner devotion, we feel this shining out of your hearts, and we come to you to assist you. You will feel our quiet words within your hearts, easing your trials, widening your understanding and helping you go forward through whatever is given you to experience with joy in your hearts. Only call on us, dear ones, in your hearts and ask for our help. We are only a thought away.

Hilarion,

3 October 2011

Introduction

HOW THIS BOOK CAME INTO BEING

This book tells a story of cosmic dimensions, of star beings, sacred lands, and shifts in consciousness. It records the messages that the Star Councils of Light wished to send to people on the Earth channelled through me as their emissary, as they term it. Here you will find their messages relating to the crop circles that they take responsibility for making in 2012 around Avebury, in Wiltshire. The area that the star beings call the sacred lands is about nine or ten miles in radius, centred on the Stone Circles of the Henge which you can see in the beautiful aerial photograph opposite.

There are many different ways of investigating the enigmatic crop circles which have appeared year after year on these lands, and many layers of meaning to them. This is not a book which will detail the exciting and painstaking scientific research on the phenomenon, nor will it analyse their geometry or decipher their codes in accordance with astronomical, mathematical or artistic means. There are many excellent books which do just that and some are mentioned in the Resources section at the back. I am most grateful to all those who have contributed their knowledge and devoted work to the recording and understanding of the crop circles over the last twenty to thirty years. The work of these dedicated researchers and photographers, has laid the basis – along with the rapidly changing times we live in - for a step into direct communication with the cosmic consciousness behind the crop circles on a larger scale than has previously happened.

For of course it has happened before, many of those who love the crop circles talk of their awareness of the consciousness that creates the circles and communicate with it through the focus of their own specialisations. It is also well-known in the crop circle world that there are many people who have personal connections to the non-human creators of crop circles, through meditation, direct inspiration and channelling. I think that the documentation and sharing of all these experiences over the years is testimony to the great all-encompassing intelligence of the cosmic beings who create the formations in the fields to communicate with us, and with whom we can connect.

It is also testimony to the cosmic aspect of the human spirit. To me we are all cosmic beings in our souls, though we may be conscious of this to widely varying degrees. I think the crop circles are clarion calls to wake up to the spiritual aspects of our being, to our Higher Selves, and to our own connections to the stars and to the cosmic dimensions beyond the 3D reality we live in on the Earth. I feel they herald the dramatic expansion in human consciousness that very many people have begun to experience since the end of 2012.

The Avebury Crop Circles and the Star Councils of Light

The main body of the book is composed of three chapters documenting the Avebury crop circle season of 2012: the early phase, April to June, then July, and August, the summer months when most of the formations arrive as the crops approach harvesting time. Each of the formations is illustrated with breath-taking aerial photographs showing the designs - from the simplest of circles to the most intricate geometrical patterns - along with ground-shots taken inside the circles revealing the patterns made as the crop was flattened and laid down, which is known as the lay. These beautiful images will greatly help the reader contemplate the transcripts of the channelled messages from the Star Councils of Light, and also help with sensing the energetic imprints of the crop circles.

I also share the story of my own higher being's involvement with the Star Councils of Light over the course of the year of 2012 and my process of integrating this growing cosmic awareness into my human consciousness. Gradually more and more aspects of how the crop circles can speak to us became clear to me as I was led deeper into the mysteries of how to decipher their star scripts with my human consciousness, in addition to what I received telepathically as a channel.

My human consciousness was ever being stretched as I integrated the knowledge gained from the spiritual initiations I was passing through, with all their attendant trials and experiences. One of the things that helped me integrate the extraordinary experiences I was having was playing my big gong which I take to the Avebury stones when possible. When I play there the great symphonic tones reverberate through me and the stones and into the ground, shaking out unsettled energies and harmonising through the sheer power of their resounding dissonances. I play by a stone in the North-West Quarter, fourth along from the road, whose being I was able to channel. She told me she was 'the Heart Stone of the whole Henge', and that she loved me to play by her so she can send the resonance of the 'Sounding Light' to reconnect not only all the stones of the circles, but all the fragments of stone that belong, whether they were in roads or houses or barns, so they might all work together again in their original vibrations.

Ancient Temple at Avebury - Painting by Peter Le Lievre (1812 – 1878 PD-Art

Avebury and the Living Mother Ship

The following message from the Star Councils of Light speaks of Avebury, the Heart Stone, and the star beings' mother ship.

The Star Councils of Light:

Avebury is the centre, for the Stone Circle at Avebury truly is the sacred centre of this landscape and holds the mother ship overhead to guard and protect the sacred places of these lands… Our mother ship is not fixed and static but is a living being comprised of living star beings and their work. All is an organic whole. Here we live in and of the Light. Our being is Light, our forms are Light, and our work is Light. Our communication is of the nature of Light and Resonance. This is why the being of the Heart Stone speaks to you of your gong playing being 'Sounding Light'. When Light and Sounding work together, then is the power to manifest and transform very great.

Re-connecting the Stones

This is why we wish you to play as often as possible in the stones for they need the healing of your Sounding Light. It lifts the vibration and allows the stones to re-tune themselves to their original notes, for they are much altered by the rituals performed within their spheres of influence.

Those rituals that are not in tune with the stones themselves, those that are imposed upon

Playing the 'Sounding Light' at the Heart Stone, Avebury   © Amuna Ra

6

them without asking of the stones, have tended to push the frequency of the stones out of kilter. This has been happening over a very long time, yet it can be righted in a much shorter 'time' due to the possibilities of now being in the Fourth Dimension. It can be righted by frequent playing of the Sounding Light, at the Heart Stone, and at the other two key points you know already. More will be made conscious in you as you continue to do this work, dear friend and colleague on the earth.

The Star Councils of Light, Spring Equinox 2013

As well as the vast mother ship which over-spans the sacred lands of Avebury, the star beings also describe their small craft as being organic, and say they can shift their forms as needed, and show themselves according to how a human being can receive them. In other words, some people may see them as more solid looking and more metallic, others will see them as balls of light, and still others experience them as pure moving energy or even as tones, as sound. The perceptions of them are affected by the consciousness of the one perceiving, as well as by the beings commanding the craft.

Healing and Helping the Earth

The Star Councils of Light speak of how the energies of their crop circles work to heal and balance the energies of everyone who enters them, and of how they work as healing medicine into the Earth to balance and hold her as she adjusts to the changes caused by the current shifts in her axis and by the increased radiation issuing from the Sun as solar flares.

They also tell of their fervent wish to assist the Earth and humanity and speak of how they wanted to announce themselves openly in the summer of 2012 only to be diverted by needing to deflect the forces of the dark. They even illustrated their desired scenario, our harmonious reception of their arrival, in one of the crop circles at the end of July. There are wonderful teachings on overcoming not only fear, but also positive expectations, both of which can hinder our ability to be completely open to the star beings, just as any preconceived judgements hinder us in meeting new people in ordinary social life.

You will find a record of how the Star Councils of Light worked to safeguard the Olympic Games in London during August and of the assistance given to them in this work by the prayers and meditations of many thousands of people on the earth. They say this was a conscious working together between human beings and the star beings on an unprecedented scale, and is a sign of our swiftly growing spiritual awakening to our cosmic origins which brings with it a heartfelt wish to connect to our Star Brothers and Sisters from this and other galaxies.

The Star Councils of Light are members of the Galactic Federation, highly evolved beings from many Star Nations who have agreed to work together on an inter-galactic level to help the highest evolution of all solar systems. They have complete respect for the free will of human beings on the Earth and wish to offer us assistance from their advanced light technology when we are ready to work with them and want to receive their help. But they have recently decided it is within their remit to *invite* us to ask them and they do so often in these pages, and when we do request their assistance in our hearts, as you will find out if you try, they are able to work strongly with us and we with them.

My Spiritual Path

My first spiritual experience was a spontaneous and quite conscious out-of the body experience where I met a great and pure Being of Light at Easter, 1976. He was full of love and the gentlest light-filled consciousness, all-wise and all-powerful. I'd grown up in an atheist family, and was at best an honest agnostic, and I had absolutely no concepts to describe this experience other than that I knew it was a living spiritual being who was the Life Force itself with whom I merged in communion. My experience was undeniable, and it changed me completely. I knew the divine did exist, and I noticed that any fear of death was quite gone, for I knew I had seen the realms beyond death. I also noticed I had a streak of white hair at my right temple, which hadn't been there before – a mark of the part of me that had died that night. I knew now from my own experience that the worlds of the spirit were real, and at the age of twenty-five, and a single mother of two, my spiritual journey had begun. I was seeking a conscious path back to the spiritual worlds that I had glimpsed and I wanted to communicate with the beings who dwell there. Since then the esoteric path of development has been the backbone of my life.

From that point on, I have felt that it was possible for us all to open to direct spiritual experience within our own consciousness, and that the spiritual path was actually a very practical one that would take us to the point where we could explore anything we wished, once we had reached the degree of discernment, self-knowledge and selflessness needed to be able to enter the higher dimensions of the spiritual worlds and know beyond doubt that our own perceptions are true.

Three years after my spiritual awakening, while living high up in the Pennines in the north of England I met people who told me of a kind of school which worked from the principle of children being spiritual beings who needed to be lovingly nurtured in order to unfold into their true individuality, rather than be taught to be a cog in the machine. I was also given a pile of books by Rudolf Steiner, 1861-1925, the Austrian spiritual teacher whose work led to the hundreds of Steiner Schools in the world today, as well as to innovations in medicine, art, science and agriculture which links to the stars (bio dynamic). Soon I had moved to Bristol to be involved in the Steiner School there.

For the next thirty years I was very active in the Steiner movement, first in teaching the youngest children in Steiner schools. It was in Bristol in the late eighties when I was studying Modern Languages that I first heard wondrous tales of the crop circles in Wiltshire from friends. I felt a strong pull, but as I was leaving for Switzerland the very next day I wasn't free to go and investigate at the time. I then spent four years studying painting at the Goetheanum, the world centre of the Steiner movement near Basel, financing my art studies by working as an English teacher and translator.

Art and Regression: Two Bridges to the Spirit

Then came a twelve year period of great joy: painting, teaching art, meditation and the path of inner development in art training colleges, running my own small painting school for a few years in Sussex, and teaching many kinds of spiritual courses and workshops in the UK and Europe from Finland to Greece.

Besides art as a bridge to the spirit, the other threads to my esoteric interests have always been reincarnation and karma, and the evolution of consciousness. I took my studies in metaphysics and human consciousness further more recently and gained a Post-Graduate Certificate in Western Esotericism from Exeter University. Then immediately, being someone who always gravitates towards an experiential approach, I trained in Past Life Regression Therapy and Spiritual Regression to the 'Life Between Lives' or inter-life state. My own memories of past lives had started to surface from my early thirties in meditation and in the tussles of life, and now I had acquired tools which worked quickly to help other people release the deep blocks on their paths and integrate their strengths from the past into the present.

But once you start going backwards through time, which is what regression is, and freely exploring the soul's existence in spiritual dimensions, it is not long before your old concepts of time dissolve altogether. You realise that just as a human being's subtle bodies – the etheric or life body, the astral body and the mental and spiritual bodies - all interpenetrate each other as well as the physical, so do all the different spiritual dimensions, and also all the different time periods we have lived in.

The Mary and Michael Stones in the Cove, Avebury   *© Amuna Ra*

From one perspective these are all aspects of the holographic sphere of consciousness, and they are definitely affected by how we focus our consciousness on them, and what we do with that focus, that is, what our intention is to create or resolve. Here the esoteric path and the path of healing meet quantum physics in the experience of the creative power of consciousness. And the new physics can prove the reality of these quantum processes, which I find highly exciting.

In the last few years I have developed my Star Journey Workshops to guide people into going back before their first lives on Earth to access their star origins, and I hold Star Connecting Courses to train people to consciously connect and communicate with the star beings and angels, and work with basic energy maintenance and soul balance. I have now worked with hundreds of clients and workshop participants, gathering myriad stories of soul experience from past lives on the earth to the interlife and existences on other planets, stars and galaxies. All the while I was observing how successive generations of younger people were bringing with them a quite different consciousness, such as that of the Indigo Children and the Star seeds. It was evident to me that there was a new and cosmic consciousness coming into general human experience.

The Significance of 2012 for 2013 and Beyond

The fourth chapter of this book, The Transition to the New Earth, speaks of the changes in consciousness that we have collectively been living through on the Earth since the end of 2012. This is why the star messages of the crop circles of 2012 have a particular significance, for they heralded the transformation to the New Earth which was born at the Winter Solstice of 2012 when the Earth came into alignment with the very centre of our galaxy for the first time in 26,000 years, a mighty turning point of the ages prophesied in many of the world's spiritual systems as a shift into an age of tremendous new potential. For example, Hinduism speaks of the advent of the Golden Age after the end of Kali Yuga, the Age of Darkness, and the Mayans recorded how their Sun God, Quetzalcoatl, would return at the end of their Long Count Calendar, which coincided with the December Solstice of 2012 and would usher in the next age.

This point of galactic alignment worked as a portal, an opening into the Fourth Dimension for the planet Earth and our Sun. Since then, the star beings say, all life on earth has existed in both the Third Dimension and the Fourth - which is the astral worlds of dream and imagination, the dimension our souls first exist in after death - and many people also have access to yet higher dimensions. Though human beings are conscious of this great shift to varying degrees, all of us are experiencing distortions in time, and circumstances becoming more fluid and malleable than heretofore, causing much confusion of expectations, but also giving us great opportunities when we learn how to navigate these new waters. This chapter offers profound and loving messages channelled from the September Equinox of 2012 until the March Equinox of 2013 which serve as guidance in steering our way through the fluidity of this newly accessible dimension of consciousness, and finding our soul balance in the processes of transition which will continue for many more years to come.

Channelling and the Call to the Crop Circles

But how did I become so deeply involved with the crop circles, after my life had taken me abroad to paint when I first felt the pull twenty years earlier? It happened one day in the summer of 2011 when I was sitting in the sun by the harbour in Brixham, Devon where I lived. I was channelling, surrounded by people eating ice-cream and fish and chips and enjoying the holiday ambience. I was conversing in my mind with a star being by the name of Peroptimé whom I knew well, when suddenly two words came in loud and distinct: 'CROP CIRCLES!'

The process of channelling can be likened to translating between earthly languages. In Switzerland I had frequently worked as a simultaneous interpreter for lectures and conferences. To instantly translate someone else's words as faithfully as possible into your own language, which may or may not hold similar concepts, is very like channelling the thoughts of a spiritual being into a human language. It only works to the extent you can clear your mind and receive what is transmitted with integrity, not losing your focus for one moment, and not allowing your own thoughts or responses to intrude. It was an excellent training for my work channelling the thoughts of cosmic beings now. Like translating, channelling can be instant and spoken aloud, or written and shared later.

There I was sitting on the bench by the water, writing in my notebook, oblivious to the crowds around me, and the words 'Crop Circles' were still sounding strongly in my mind, I asked Peroptimé if he wanted to speak with me about crop circles, and he replied mysteriously, 'No, but my brother does.' His brother announced that he came from the far off stars of Andromeda and that his name was Anaximander. When I responded conversationally that his name sounded Greek to me, he told me in no uncertain terms in his slow strong voice, 'It may sound Greek to you, but it is Andromedan.'

He then informed me that it was time for me to be in a fresh crop circle that season and they wished me to prepare to leave for Avebury straight away. It was July, the summer holidays, and my grandchildren were coming to stay with me by the sea, so it was a week before I could set off in my camping van on the journey that would change my life once more.

This is one of the beautiful crop circle made by the Pleiadians in which I was delighted to spend a lot of happy and fruitful time in those last warm weeks of summer.

Star Dance, Knoll Down - 13 August 2011   *© Steve Alexander*

Less than nine months later, I had bought a house and moved to live near Avebury, just thirteen days before the first crop circle of 2012 arrived. I was poised to be able to visit nearly all of the crop circles that would appear in the surrounding areas, and honoured to be able to channel the messages from the star beings I am sharing with you here.

Conversing with a Star Being on Crop Circles and the Shift

To give you another taste of what channelled conversations with star beings can be like, here are the words of a being new to me, who contacted me in the autumn of 2011. When I asked his name, he announced himself as Almeron. I think it is always important to know something about who you are talking with, so I asked if I might ask him where he came from and what his star lineage was. This preamble also gives you both time to adjust your frequencies and for you to sense whether the vibrations are compatible. Any being of the light will tell you straightforwardly who they are, and you will hear what they say as long as your frequency is clear enough to receive the response. If there is any hesitation I know to be wary, for there are as many different kinds of beings out there as there are different kinds of people on the Earth.

Almeron:

You may ask this. I come from the stars known as Seinta. They are a long way off. My star lineage is that of the tribe of Almera. I speak for my brothers and sisters of Almera. I speak to you for you can hear me. We need people who can hear us, so our work may be understood as well as felt. The impressions of our formations work into the earth and help the recalibration be on track. We recalibrate the human beings also. But most are unaware of what is happening to them. They feel the energy but do not know just what we do. So they do not meet us with the necessary consciousness and they do not hear our words to know what they must do. For we can give but one part of the shift, the other is dependent on the freedom of the human being to acknowledge us and work with us. When a human being awakes to our presence in real consciousness, not only in the dream of feeling, then the communication is two ways. We can work strongly with such a human being. And we wish many more to fully awaken and to work with us in consciousness.

We need colleagues upon the earth, star beings in human bodies. For those who have been very long upon the earth like you, dear Amuna Ra, it may take a long time to wake up to your starry activities. But when you do awaken then the power is full and strong and we can work with you as one. For those others who wake more quickly but have less experience on the earth, our activity may be more curtailed until they accept their earthly role in understanding. You can help with these processes in those who come towards you. We will work through you when you channel us, dear star sister.

Almeron, 3 September 2011

Star Connecting on Silbury Hill

But the beginning of my telepathic connection to the star beings was two years earlier in early August 2009 when I slept on top of Silbury Hill. That night was when I was first contacted by the Star Councils of Light of the Galactic Federation. I was told in a most loving way that I was a member of the Star Councils of Light in my higher being and that I would be preparing myself for joint work with them. There would be many changes within me, on all levels of my being, which would clear and purify my energy channels, but for now all I needed was to make myself 'very comfortable.' As the top of Silbury Hill is hard and stony that took some doing, all I could think of was to imagine the surface beneath me dissolving and softening. And as I did this, I found myself sinking down in my inner experience and entering white cavernous spaces within the chalky structure. I did sleep, and very comfortably! I later realised that if

I made myself very comfortable on all levels, at all times, I would fit myself for anything needed in life, because I would be caring for myself fully and would function optimally. The phrase 'Make yourself very comfortable' has become a mantra which accompanies me.

Silbury Hill, from the top of West Kennett Long Barrow © *Amuna Ra*

That summer I had been experiencing a great expansion in my spiritual awareness as one phase of my life was drawing to a close. I had received meditations from Hilarion for some years and channelled him regularly, but I had never thought of consciously working with beings from the stars before. Now I found myself drawn to working with people who did, and my own opening to the starry realms and to channelling the star beings was rapid. I had been seriously involved in meditation and the esoteric since that first spiritual awakening in my mid-twenties, but for the first few decades I had had little notion of star beings.

Past Life Regression to Egypt

Except that a few years previously I had experienced a powerful and detailed past life initiation in Ancient Egypt in a three hour regression session with a colleague. This was the last in a series of long regressions to an Egyptian life when I had been a Queen and High Priestess in the 18th Dynasty who was fully clairvoyant and completely connected to the gods and to the starry realms. Part of my work was in the training of priestesses in the temple to follow the souls of the dead on their journeys into the after-life; I knew the processes of embalming and the rituals needed to safeguard the souls as they made the transition into the after-life in the stars. Part was in the focussing of cosmic energy through the uraeus, the undulating cobra-form worn on the brow, so it might be used in the wise ruling of the Two Lands through allowing the divine power to flow out to serve the needs of the land and the people. Another part of my work was connected with the temple building, when groups of priests and priestesses would focus the cosmic rays from the stars to alter the relationship of the great blocks of stone to the Earth's gravity, making them easier to raise than present day science suspects was possible, for light has the property of lessening density as well as illuminating.

My life was shared between the Temple and Court and family responsibilities - it was very important to bear lots of children as in all dynasties. The rhythm of life in an Egyptian Temple is one of great veneration for the life forces, observance of the daily rituals of honouring the gods at dawn and noon and sunset, and of the passage through the successive initiations into higher states of consciousness in the great festivals of the year. Awareness of the stars was everywhere, painted on all the ceilings of the temples and carved on the pillars of the great courts which were in turn painted in beautiful colours. The loving adoration of life, humanity and the divine was palpable all around.

Star Origins in the Pleiades

The Egyptians felt that the souls of the dead existed in the stars 'for all eternity,' and one of the ways we have today to enter the timeless zones in which our souls dwell between lives on Earth or elsewhere in the cosmos is regression. Through guided visualisation into an altered state of consciousness on the cusp of waking and sleeping, the regression process leads us to be able to perceive and experience our soul's existence in other times and other realms.

In my regression I re-lived what had transpired in the Egyptian times and became conscious of the working between High Priestess/Queen and the starry realms, and of how the star knowledge was transferred in a bright shaft of light into the mind of the Queen sitting in the Chamber of Initiation.

Then the experience morphed into an initiation of my present-day consciousness. In this second stage, I consciously journeyed back to my origins in the Pleiades, to my home on Alcyone and learned to know my star lineage. I felt absolutely comfortable

The stars of the Pleiades, Alcyone is the brightest star in the centre   Hubble Telescope/PD

as a distinctly blue being of light, a blue sphere of conscious energy. There were many of us, and we travelled along lines of vibrant coloured light, called by resonance, the tones sounding across vast distances. Travel was instant and effected simply by thought. There was no separation between thinking and doing, it was one and the same - all thought was immediate creation.

And it was this same creative power of the stars which guided the ruling of the land in Egypt through the King and Queen and the priesthood, who were divine messengers and interpreters for the will of the gods, and the star beings who stood behind the gods as their higher beings. This was so, that is, while the star connection remained unbroken in Egypt, for there came a time when this changed and the culture thereafter slowly degenerated, making way for the beginning of modern times and individual thinking which was marked by the love of philosophy and art in Ancient Greece, and by the organisational force of Rome.

But it was this initiatory experience of travelling to the Pleiades on the inner planes in the regression, that gave me my first taste of what it could be like to be a star being, and since then I have often remembered how much I have loved the stars of the Pleiades in this life. I would stand outside as a child of eleven after I had first had them pointed out to me and gaze up at the Seven Sisters, as the Pleiades are called. On clear frosty nights I could see their twinkling colours distinctly, but I never got seven however hard I tried to count them. And I would think of them being so very far away.

The Star Beings You Meet Here, and their Angelic Names

In the course of this book, you will meet several of the star beings who work in the Star Councils of Light through their words. You will get to know Peroptimé, the star being from the Andromedan Galaxy, who frequently acts as the spokesperson for the Star Councils of Light. It was he who was speaking with me by the harbour in Brixham, and he has since shared the information that in his angelic form he is known as the Archangel Sandalphon.

From the high angelic ranks, Metatron, who works very closely with the Star Councils of Light, also speaks in his star being aspect as Anaximander of Andromeda, a correlation revealed to me only after the 2012 crop circle season was over. Peroptimé had told me they were brothers, and we find that in Jewish and Christian lore, the Archangels

Metatron and Sandalphon are regarded as twins[i]. But you will find that the names Metatron and Anaximander are juxtaposed most carefully in the crop circle channelling to do with Metatron's Cube at Hackpen Hill of 26 August 2012, for I did not then know they were one and the same being.

You will find messages and guidance from the great spiritual master, Hilarion, who in his star origins hails from Sirius. The spiritual teachers who are known as Ascended Masters have all had incarnations upon the Earth, and have risen in their spiritual development on the spirals of initiation, to the state of enlightenment and a full consciousness of their higher being and their cosmic mission. In his last earthly incarnation as Rudolf Steiner, 1861-1925, Hilarion worked strongly to prepare the way for the great shift in consciousness we are living through now.

The star identity of my great esoteric teacher through the ages, Melchisedek, was also made known to me before I finished writing. He revealed that he is Sirius Ra, who speaks for the Sirian High Command in the Star Councils of Light, and in this book alternates his use of names in the messages through the winter of transition of 2012 to 2013, again it was some time before I knew they were two names of the same being.

You will meet Wasaki, one of my beloved companions in my star being form. He it was who first called me to my work with the Galactic Federation on top of Silbury Hill, informing me he was the Commander of the Fleet, and from the Andromedan Galaxy. Like others of the star beings, he is known by the name of one of his closest associations to human beings. In his case this was when he appeared as the Mayan Sun-god, Kukulcan or Quetzalcoatl, the Feathered Serpent. He normally uses this name when I channel him in relation to the crop circles, as it is familiar to many people. Whenever I have inwardly seen Wasaki in his star being form, I see him as a thin little silvery grey being with a large head and beautiful big dark shining eyes, full of love. For those who may wish to know, this being's angelic name is Raguel.

And you will also meet Amuna Ra, my Higher Self or Star Self. She sometimes calls me her 'counterpart on the earth', and I trust you will be able to find your way through the unusual use of pronouns which result from our telepathic conversations. Amuna Ra's Pleiadian star body is similar to Wasaki's, but a deep blue in colour, with a purply blush like a damson, with head and large eyes very like his. I see her as about 4'6" tall (about 1.4 metres). One of the roles I have in my higher being is as a Keeper of the Records, and I share with you here Metatron's response to my request for more detail of what this means.

A Keeper of the Records

Metatron:

Oh, Amuna Ra, a Keeper of the Records is one who watches over the Akasha and is concerned with the balances in the universe. These balances are karmic balances and energetic balances within the star systems of the universe. In relation to the Planet Earth, you, as a Keeper of the Records, observe the activities within the earth as she shifts and within the human beings as they shift in their inner development. Hence your outer tasks have always reflected this within your human embodiments.

As for your work in the City of Light, it is to do with cosmic rays and re-balancing the forces of the earth as she is recalibrated. You monitor the changes and give instruction to the light ships who are concerned with the starry imprints upon the body of Gaia which you humans call crop circles. Yours is the responsibility of fine tuning the earth's responses to her birthing pangs. You administer, through your colleagues, the correct medicines to assist dear Gaia in the changes she is undergoing. It could be expressed as you being the consultant who directs the doctors who give the medicine to the body of Gaia.

Metatron, 2 March 2012.

These are portentous words and they were to take some time to be assimilated into my mind, but they probably went some way towards preparing me for my first major experience of the 'City of Light' five weeks after I came to live near Avebury. In regard to my developing consciousness of my star connection, so far I knew that my star origins were on the Pleiades long ago. I am aware it is a very long time ago, for I know my soul has been incarnating on the Earth for about 400,000 years and I feel deeply bound to this planet's evolution. I also knew from meditative experiences in 2009 that my Higher Self name is Amuna Ra (I began to use this name in my professional life then, and Amuna has now become my name in everyday life too) and I was channelling conversations with my Higher Self and being given knowledge of my simultaneous existence as a star being. The peak moment of this process was the reception of my higher being into myself which took place on a wild and stormy night in May 2012, on top of the hill at Cherhill between Calne and Avebury.

The City of Light

In my morning meditation I was asked to go up Cherhill, which is just a few miles from where I live, at 10 pm 'whatever the weather' as the Star Councils of Light wished to meet with me. I could inwardly see the spot, directly above the White Horse by the trees and I checked out a route during the day, for I had not been up there before. It was very wet and windy with cloud hanging low when I climbed up in the dark, not using a torch as I love to experience the darkness of night. I made my way to the top and waited, not knowing quite for what.

At precisely 10 o'clock, I saw a great number of lights in the sky high up and over to the north appearing out of the thick cloud, bright and shining like a great Celestial City. And I knew in my heart that this *was* what it was: it was the Celestial City spoken of by mystics of old, and I knew it also to be the City of Light, the mother ship where I work with my colleagues in my star being form. I felt exalted, and gloried in the wondrous sight for ten minutes or more and then began to move towards it, with an increasing longing in my heart to go to it. I came to a halt where the rough ground sloped down rapidly, and suddenly saw several of spheres of light coming quickly towards me from the east and through the trees. They got bigger as they neared me and one came straight towards me, about two feet across, and I knew it to be the Light of my Soul - my Higher Self, my Star Self - entering right into me.

Overcoming Doubt

Afterwards I was slightly dazed, and then realised I was alone in the storm, and not long before had been talking out loud with a great longing in my heart to meet with my star being colleagues, which now didn't seem to have happened as I had hoped. I thought for a moment that if anyone could see me they would think I was crazy. And the minute that doubt crossed my mind, the glory and wonder was abruptly over. I began to think that the City of Light - which I could still see quite clearly - must be a village with streetlights and lighted windows over in the north. I felt a heavy disappointment and began to trudge down the hill, thinking how foolish I had been.

When I got home, I connected with the Star Councils of Light and my Star Self answered, saying, 'How *could* you believe and then not believe?' She genuinely could not understand what had happened, so I patiently outlined how my human mind had worked, and she said I should get out the map the next day and see that there was no village at that height anywhere to the north of Cherhill.

The next morning I found this was true. There was nothing at that altitude, not even any high ground, for what I had seen was much higher than the spot where I was standing above the White Horse, and to the north there was no village or large farm or anything that could possibly have been lit up to the extent I had seen. The village of Cherhill itself is much lower down and has no streetlights except along the main road.

Union with my Higher Self

Sheer logic was now suggesting to me that what I had seen was not in three-dimensional reality. It still took the best part of three weeks for the residue of the doubt to dissipate completely and leave me free to absorb what the star beings were telling me had happened: that my Higher Self - Amuna Ra, my Star Self - had descended and united herself with me, merged with me. She, my Star Self, still had the capacity to split her being and work in various other locations as needed, of which my human mind was not conscious. All in all it seemed best to continue to address her as a being separate from myself since we each still had our individuality as well as this new-found unity. Words and grammar do not easily encompass this kind of spiritual merging; besides we could have some beautifully enlightening conversations that way!

Slowly the wonder returned as I remembered the glory I had been graced with in seeing the illumination of the City of Light, and I was most grateful for it. By the time the image of the City of Light appeared in a crop circle at the end of June at Stanton St. Bernard on page 69, I had come to terms with my experience, though not yet with many of the ramifications of being conscious of part of my being working aboard the mother ship. I describe this process of spiritual experience, subsequent doubt and the overcoming of it, as I am now meeting other people who are having experiences of their star counterparts in one way or another, and are often finding it extremely hard to adjust to what they know in their souls and integrate it into their lives. It becomes easier as we expand our concepts and have the courage to speak about them and embrace the new paradigms more fully. Then we can begin to accept that we ourselves exist on many levels, in many dimensions, and that parallel lives or simultaneous existences are no longer merely the stuff of science fiction. And as this new awareness becomes assimilated into our being, we find it strengthens us greatly.

Chapter Five is a short drawing together of further aspects of the integration process, along with more on signature glyphs, star codes and the awakening of star being consciousness. And the book concludes with a very unexpected revelation in the PPS.

Initiations in Consciousness

Writing this book in order to share it with those who wish to understand, has been a help in my own integrating of the trials and initiations I have passed through since I came to live on the magical lands of Avebury in April 2012, and in my deeper understanding of the spirals of the spiritual path, and what it means to literally 'reach for the stars'.

And if it all still seems very far-fetched to others of you, please read this book as a story, as science-fiction if you will. The star beings are happy for everyone to read their words in any way you wish to take them in, and what they want to say will percolate into the collective consciousness as more and more people become familiar with their loving intent through their own experience or through their words – for they are speaking through many channels at this time. They are delighted by everyone who takes any kind of real interest, for they wish nothing more than eventually to work openly with human beings, and to share their highly evolved light technology with us when we are ready to receive it, so that we human beings may be able to overcome our problems ourselves, utilise the free energy and the resources available to us, and live in peace on this beautiful planet.

The Avebury Crop Circle Messages

The process of gathering together all the crop circles that appeared in the nine miles or so around Avebury, and only those, has been incredibly exciting as it revealed a pattern of messages and signs in their starry script that I hadn't seen on the ground at the time or in the aerial photographs. Of the crop circles that the Star Councils of Light claimed as their own in 2012, there were thirty six from April to August, three times twelve, three times the number of the year of completion, 2012, and then there was added the one which arrived extraordunarily late, in mid-October at Windmill Hill, to remain and carry the energy of transformation all through the autumn and winter and into 2013.

I began to understand more and more of how the star beings communicate with us as human beings. They had told me early in the season that they would alert me to where they were going to make a new formation, but it wasn't until fairly late in August that I began to recognise *how* they were doing this: that they were showing me with lines of direction which pointed to where the next crop circles would appear. As you read on through the sequence of the crop circles and look at the exquisite beauty of the forms revealed in the

In the Flower of Life, Avebury - 1
August 2012   © Amuna Ra

aerial photography, you will be accompanying me in my gradual awakening to what was going on over the course of 2012, the year in our planet's evolution that marked the transition of both the Earth and the Sun into the Fourth Dimension. And there will no doubt be many more revelations to come in the future as more and more people awaken to the opportunities of the new possibilities of access to higher dimensions.

Most of the crop circle channelling was done within the formations or when I returned home after spending several hours in them. Sometimes while compiling the book, fresh conversations opened up with the Star Councils of Light as I suddenly had a new insight, for to them - and to me while in telepathic communication - all this was taking place in a space of 'no time' - the crop circles of 2012, my experiences and reactions to them at the time and my writing in the early months of 2013.

The star beings were ever amused at the 'slowness' of my human mental processes, as they were also ever patiently reminding me that in my higher being I work as a colleague alongside them in the City of Light, the mother ship, and that in that parallel reality all that is contained in this book is 'all in a day's work' for me. I was grateful for their constant kindly patience and humour as my human consciousness continually stretched to encompass the enormity of these cosmic perspectives.

Discovering the Codes of the Crop Circles

Alongside the channelled messages of the star beings about the crop circles of 2012 around Avebury in the next section of the book, there unfolds the parallel story of my discoveries and energetic experiences in the formations themselves. You will see that it was a path of gradual realisation, of solving mysteries and puzzles and being led step by step, and of ultimate acceptance of the reality of my Higher Self existing as a star being in another dimension very close to the earth.

It became very clear that asking questions is an art form in itself, for not only must a question be asked for an answer to be revealed, but the nature of the answer will depend on the consciousness behind the question, just as in quantum physics it is now well recognised that the observer affects the experiment. This factor could well contribute towards why the crop circle consciousness can seem to mean different things to different people who all have a genuine love of the formations. From a quantum point of view this is not necessarily a contradiction. We could all have a direct connection to these mysteries in our higher beings, and still bring forth diverse aspects through our specialisations and human predilections.

And yet, just as there is a distinct form to a crop circle which, while it can be interpreted in many ways - is generally agreed upon to be a circle or a cube or whatever - I believe there is a distinct form to the various beings whose consciousness creates these crop circles, and in time when more of us can perceive these beings, I have a feeling that it will be generally agreed upon as to what and who we are relating to.

It is my hope that this book will be an encouragement to others who choose to pursue the path of conscious communication with the non-human [ii] creators of the crop circles, so they will form their own questions and find the will-power and perseverance to attune their own bodies, their own instruments, to the frequencies that will enable them to perceive the answers for themselves. Then they will have come into communication with the star beings and the other spiritual beings who are waiting for our consciousness to expand to this point, the point of recognising ourselves as multi-dimensional beings.

The star beings assure us that they hold us in their hearts and dearly wish for the day that we humans will welcome them as our star brothers and sisters. The more of us who open to our own star connections, the nearer that day will be.

May these messages from the Star Councils of Light and the starry wonder of the crop circles inspire you as you read on!

From Polar Clock

to

City of Light

April - June

TWELVE-PETALLED FLOWER

Hill Barn, East Kennett - 15 April 2012

© Steve Alexander

The 2012 season began in mid-April with this delightful circle imprinted in the bright yellow flowers of canola on the brow of the hillside at Hill Barn, above East Kennett. It was a perfect circle of twelve large petals, with twelve inner petals showing a little darker in the centre.

Peroptimé, for the Star Councils of Light:

The first circle of the year that we send to you is a twelvefold flower for this twelfth year of the millennium. It is a simple flower in the field of yellow flowers to remind you of the bright shining of the sun which

32

gives you life. When you walk into the field and smell the intense fragrance and receive the yellow dust that is the flowers' gift to you. You are imbued with the qualities of these flowers. You are lifted into the world of flowers through their essence which you breathe in. You are transported into a wonderland of yellow, for is this not a most magnificent colour, dear ones? It lifts you into your spirit and you are raised up thereby. Your mind becomes clear and your emotions settle in the purity of these yellow flowers. It can be almost overwhelming for some of you when you are not used to the intensity of such an experience of yellow. But it brings you great joy, does it not, to walk in a field of yellow flowers?

The Wheel of Twelve

And when you gaze upon the pictures from the air you see the perfection of the design, the simplicity of the twelvefold form of the petals with the deepening of the impression in the centre. Your soul is drawn into the centre by the darker colours and you access your own centre with more ease. We wish you to be aware of the wheel of twelve, the number of completeness, echoed in your human reckoning of the months in the year, in the signs of the zodiac, and in the Twelve who learned from the One who came at the beginning of your measure of this era of time.

This is the first year of the twelve and it will herald much in the way of completion for all of you. You will come full cycle and be able to see yourself with greater clarity as you focus within and look upon what is a bit darker in your centre. You will go through processes of releasing what you no longer need as easily as the yellow dust wafts into the air around you, when you are as free as the flowers. This work of completion belongs to the year of the twelve.

Imprinted into the Life Forces of the Earth

My Star Self shared these words with me about how the healing forces work through the forms of this circle into the living being of the Earth, who supports our life. She speaks also about the transformation our planet was passing through in the year of 2012 and of how the rhythm of twelve would work as a medicine to help balance her through the birth to come.

Amuna Ra-Star Self, for the Star Councils of Light:

We made this circle, dear ones, to lift you into the world of joy and to imprint the circle of twelve into the etheric forces of the earth your mother. For this is the year that she is completing her birthing into the new realms, and we seek to give her the balancing doses that she needs. In this formation the rhythm of twelve is impressed deeply into her life forces and this aids her, just as your homeopathic medicines aid you if you are unbalanced.

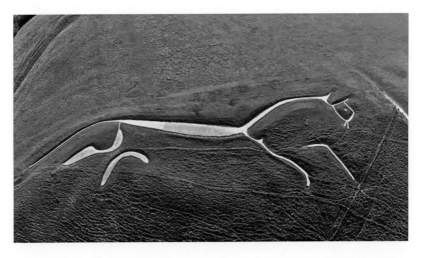

The White Horse or Dragon at Uffington   *© Steve Alexander*

SOLAR FLARES AND SUNSPOTS

Dragon's Hill, Uffington - 19 May 2012

© Steve Alexander

This little formation appeared about a month later in the field across the road from the White Horse at Uffington, which you can just see on the top of the hill. I have included it here although more than ten miles from Avebury as I think there is a vital connection between the two places. This chalk carving is at least 3000 years old and is much more a depiction of an ancient dragon than a horse. I feel it illustrates the old knowledge of the serpent energies of the earth coursing along the grids of leylines connecting the sacred places of this land.

The content of the star messages given here are also important for the themes that will be developed in this book, for it was here that my star being colleagues asked me to write about each crop circle I went to. You will be able to see also how they often work with me in a crop circle, speaking now to me personally, now in a broad general discourse, then giving me healing or balancing and later returning to the themes of the formation.

I was sitting in the small inner circle on the left in the aerial photo, feeling wonderfully comfortable and at home in the energy. When the conversation began it was my star being self who responded, and the pronouns were consequently a little confusing. I trust you the reader will bear with the grammatical complexities arising from my relationship with the other aspects of my being. I had enquired simply why this circle was so delightful to me; she answered me and then took the opportunity of my having pen in hand to address all human beings in a wide-ranging discourse.

Pleiadian Energy

Amuna Ra, Star Self:

It's because it belongs to you, created with my-your energy, oh Amuna Ra. You feel at home, because you are at home. It is a little bit of your home and calls to all who belong to Alcyone, and to all Pleiadians. By experiencing it, human beings can know what Pleiadian energy is. They can feel our love, feel our open gesture and learn to relate to us. This circle faces into the epicentre - which is slightly off-centre - as that is the way the communication goes, from the stars to your sun. The epicentre being not yet truly centred is the problem. We spoke before about the sunspots which you can observe with your physical instruments. The unusual heightened activity on and in the sun is causing imbalance on the earth. The axes are shifting and you experience disturbances in your weather systems. The sun is shifting in her cosmic orbit also, and there is nothing to be done other than go through these shifts along with your Mother Earth and Father Sun.

Transformations to Come

Each one of you will have the choice as to how they experience the transformations to come. It will depend on your inner attitudes. If you have done sufficient inner work on yourself to have become fluid and flexible and yet steadfast and strong, you will bend with the winds and spring back again and continue your growing, like the yellow flowers of the fields. Rigidities will meet insurmountable force and be damaged. So, dear ones, the choice is yours: to 'go with the flow' as you say – but not unconsciously – or to suffer with the storms which break out upon your planet, both climatic and man-made catastrophes. Do not expect to be plucked out and lifted to another dimension with no effort on your part. On the contrary, we need you to play your part and come to meet us. As you transform yourselves, so you enter the higher dimensions where we can work together and be co-creators of the cosmic future of the planet. The higher dimensions are none other than states of consciousness.

Stretch your Minds

Dear ones, open up your minds and awake on higher levels. Stretch your consciousness and feel our love as your hearts open also. We will always help those who reach towards us with an open heart and unprejudiced mind. For we long to work openly alongside you. For this we must await your readiness, for we need to be invited.

Thus we send you our messages in the flowers and the corn. Come into them and renew your energy, for there is surplus for each one of you. The formations send our love and assistance deep into Gaia and she in turn allows all who enter to share in this abundance. We can help you in the passage through the months ahead by recharging you and recalibrating you in the crop formations, for they are our script for all who dwell upon the earth, and within her.

Receiving Energy

You are feeling now the force of the energy surging through you, Amuna Ra. It is like being plugged into your home so far off on Alcyone. You feel the strength of the energy pulsing up through your Stars Within *(this is what they call our chakras)* enlivening and activating you, dear one. And an activated Amuna Ra on the earth is what we need to do our work. Feel the energy strengthening you and rising up, now in your sun-power centre. We need you powerful and conscious of your own power. Shyness does not suit a blue star being. Gentleness and loving kindness, yes, but not shyness...

Looking towards the White Horse across the yellow flowers of the field   © *Amuna Ra*

This made me smile - they are not averse to teasing me . She continued to work with me until I had received sufficient energy, at which point she told me to lie down over the centre as they wished to heal my back. I received a gentle healing and adjustment to the whole of my spine and into my neck and head, the energy then rising up and out of my crown. The healing energies were sung to me in descending cadences by star beings from Arcturus, and it felt like a wonderfully subtle chiropractic healing and lasted twenty minutes. Then when a cramp started in my leg, they gave me new dietary guidance, saying that it was vital to sense the changing needs of my body, and give it just what it needs at each moment and not get stuck in a pattern of eating.

After the treatment had settled, I moved to the outer small circle, bottom left in the picture. It had two clockwise off-centre whorls, one with a big standing bouquet of flowers and one with a single stalk only.

Solar Flares and Sunspots

Peroptimé, for the Star Councils of Light:

Oh dear one, you sit in the outer circle which touches and borders upon the boundary of the large ring around the central circle. This is like a sunspot erupting on the surface of the sun: two uncentred whorls of activity at different velocities. Turbulent energy – spilling out and being ejected... The fall-out affects the earth as all other planets in your solar system. And more far-reaching is this activity: way beyond your solar system do the ripples of turbulence roll.

You sit at the interface of this ejection of energy within the aura of the sun. For you, it warms and energises, and you love the outward thrusting force. For some, it will feel violent. Thus do human beings differ in their capacity to endure the solar frequencies. You must acknowledge the great fieriness within you and let it out like this beautiful fountain of flames before you *(he was referring to the bright yellow flowers still standing in the centre)* by speaking and writing of your experiences. Then will the fiery flames of your power rise and you will stand tall like the unbent stalks. Write a comment about each crop circle you visit. Be our ambassador that you truly are, dear one. This is why we brought you here. You have the skills, we wish you to use them, dear one.

POLAR CLOCK

Manton Drove - 2 June 2012

Note the humour of the polar clock right beside a telegraph pole! © *Steve Alexander*

I met a young couple coming out, when I first went into this field of young barley on a very wet day just after it was reported. They had never been in a crop circle before and the man asked me if I thought it was genuine. As I hadn't yet reached the circle, I asked what he had made of it himself. His face was shining, and he said he just had to go straight to the centre and that he 'felt really calm and serene' in there. I said to him I thought he should trust his own feeling and experience, for that seemed very genuine to me.

The energy in the formation was beautifully vibrant. The stalks were not broken, just bent over with some already springing back into the vertical. There was a small tight knot of twisted stalks, bent but unbroken, right next to the standing tuft in the centre. In effect there were two centres, and when I am in the energy field of such a double centre, I usually sense a certain ambivalence or turbulence in the message of the formation.

Small tight knot and standing tuft in centre. ©Amuna Ra

What I found exciting in this formation as I was walking round was how the wave of laid stalks surged round from the narrow arcs *(top left in picture on left)* to meet the broad arcs, then abruptly changed direction at right angles to go sweeping down and round through the broad curve to where it ended. It woke you up as you turned to follow the main flow which rushed on. This made it feel difficult to double back and walk against the stream, for in each broad arc you got carried right through by the momentum of the lay to the point where it ended, where the movement - and you - came abruptly to a halt. There was no mistaking the destination to which you were led.

Narrow arc meeting broad arc at right angles

You can follow this momentum in the main aerial photograph by imagining yourself walking round the first narrow arc from the bottom, starting at the right and following the curve slowly all the way round, until at the top of the picture you suddenly find yourself facing an open space, the narrow curving pathway becomes a very broad one, and when you walk on round in the same now broad curve you arrive at a complete dead-end. You are led to this unmistakeable destination.

When I got home and dried out, I read the first comments on Crop Circle Connector[iii] about it being a polar clock, which indicated a specific time and date, the consensus of opinion seeming to be that it pointed to 7.45 pm on Saturday 4 August.

Polar Clock

I had not heard the term polar clock before, so I did some research, firstly on the internet. Wikipedia has an interesting biography of Charles Wheatstone the inventor of the polar clock in the mid-19th century,[iv] which was a device for the measuring of time using the polarised rays of light in the sky at an angle of 90 from the sun, parallel to the earth's axis. There is also a current popular usage of the polar clock as a computer screen saver image.

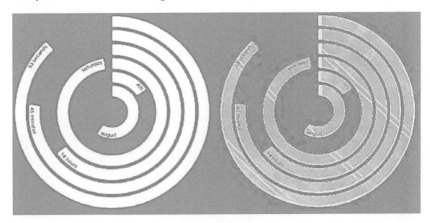

Polar Clock from inner ring: August, 4th, Saturday, 19 hours, 45 minutes, 53 seconds

I was really struck by seeing that the dead ends - the unmistakeable destinations I had arrived at by following the energetic momentum of the arcs - was the straight line made by the beginnings of the six rings indicating the date and time. The energy of the formation led me to just where the information about the date and time was to be revealed to those who could read the script.

I also did my own research on spiritual levels through direct channelling. It was Wasaki - Quetzalcoatl, the Star Being who first contacted me in 2009, who responded. I was already aware he was behind some of the crop formations at the end of last season. I asked if it was a polar clock and if so what it signified. This is his reply:

Forewarning for the Olympic Games

Wasaki-Quetzalcoatl:

Oh Amuna Ra, dear one, it *is* called a polar clock in your world. We send it to you to alert you to the events which will take place on this date on the Earth, for we wish to forewarn you. There will be cataclysmic events on this day, caused by terrorism. People will lose their lives, and there will be much disruption of services. These events are orchestrated to cause fear amongst you, and to distract you from the cosmic events which are also unfolding.

We call on you to resist the fear, and to hold to what you know and perceive as the reality of our communications. Many will need your help and clarity in this period ahead. Do not deny your own experience in our circles. When they are fresh the energy is very strong. It will heal you and awaken you to the reality of our presence and love for you human beings upon the earth.

You human beings have an unfortunate capacity for doubt, even when your inner experience is strong and true. This doubt is used by the dark forces to unsettle and un-nerve you. It must be resisted. Trust your own experience and speak out, dear ones, for you who experience our love and grace through the formations in the corn are much needed to spread clarity and steadfastness in the human population in the coming times.   *4 June 2012*

This was two months prior to the date indicated, and in posting the message, I was trusting that a forewarning would work against its worst fulfilment if enough people were to take it on board. I received several emails and comments about the message. Some worried that it would cause fear to publicise such a warning. I feel there is a fine line between ignoring the workings of the dark forces - effectively putting our heads in the sand - thus allowing them to work unhindered, and being so aware of them that our attention serves to feed them with energy, the energy of what is really our fear.

I believe it is vital that we are conscious of the existence of the dark forces, and that we choose to use our power actively to shine the light of our consciousness onto it, and send the love of our hearts to where it is needed. Both consciousness and love transform. When we do this as a conscious co-working with the forces of light and for the good, there is no danger of our succumbing to fear, for we know we are working out of our own great strength as well as being held in the arms of the beings of light, the star beings we have chosen to align ourselves with.

Questions for Quetzalcoatl

The first emailed query for Quetzalcoatl was could he be more specific: was it UK time? and are the proposed attacks in the U.K. or elsewhere?

Quetzalcoatl:

Oh dear one, the time assumed is correct, for the formation is in 'UK time'. We cannot always be as specific as you dear humans would like, but we will say that the assumptions to do with the date of 4 August and the world events going on in the UK have some validity. There is a U.S. connection to the date also. (*It is President Obama's birthday.*)

We wish to forewarn you to stimulate your awareness of the dark forces, not to stimulate your fear. How you respond to our message will show the ease with which you will come into your own power to work with the forces of light. We wish to be of assistance in your conscious awakening.

Quetzalcoatl, 8 June 2012

With these questions we can note how important it is to actually ask, so that the spiritual beings can bring the information through, and how the response also takes into account the feeling and motivation lying behind the question. Next came a plea from a woman in Stuttgart to ask Quetzalcoatl what we could *do* to not let an attack manifest, and suggesting that we start working together with a joint visualisation, even just the two of us.

Quetzalcoatl:

The dear one who asks what you can do, has the right approach to this possible event. If you gather your thoughts and meditations together the power is increased very greatly. Set a time and date to meditate with us, and the Star Councils of Light will activate your prayers for an amelioration of the events we foresaw. Your holding the time we spoke of in the light of your love will be of great assistance.

Quetzalcoatl, 14 June 2012

So I invited people widely to join with us in meditation each Saturday evening - or whenever possible - to hold the Olympic events and everyone connected with them in the love of our hearts. Then we would do the meditation every evening during the Olympics, with special focus on the weekend of 4 and 5 August. This was the beginning of working on an increasingly large scale over the seven Saturdays before 4 August to support the work of the Star Councils of Light in protecting the Olympics with the beautiful meditation that follows.

MEDITATION for the OLYMPICS

Dearest ones, centre yourselves in your hearts, and feel the Love that is there for all humankind...

Feel that Love radiating out, shining out...   till you are shining like a bright star, far out into the cosmos...

We will see your Light, dear ones, and hear the prayers of your hearts...

Hold the world events in London and everyone connected with them in the Light of your Love...

See your Love flowing out and enfolding the whole city... and call on the Star Councils of Light to send their assistance wherever it is needed... in the UK, the US, and elsewhere on your dear planet...

And rest in the peace of your hearts, dear ones... trusting that all will be done that the Power of Love and Light can bring about in your world.

We are with you always, and hold you in our love.

The Star Councils of Light

14 June 2012

We were not alone in working spiritually for the holding of the safety and harmony of the Olympic Games, other channels heard the call (though we did not know of each other in the early days and weeks) and we were joined in meditation by many thousands of Lightworkers the world over. You will see later in this book how Metatron and Hilarion describe the distinct and important energetic effect of this concentrated focus of meditation and love.

So in this way, once it had been decoded by those who could read it, the enigmatic Polar Clock crop circle at Manton Drove served as one of the great calls to focus the meditations and prayers of countless human beings in a conscious working alongside the Star Councils of Light - to ensure that the world events of the Olympic Games would unfold harmoniously in the summer of 2012.

A week later, three delightful baby dragons appeared wriggling their way across the field at Woodborough Hill. Note the little wings at the neck and at tail levels, and the eye-like form in the heads. Dragons or serpents were to become a recurring motif in the 2012 circles around Alton Barnes and Woodborough, the dragons growing larger as time went on till August brought a whole family of dragons who nested peacefully for several weeks right by the Henge at Avebury. This first formation of little dragons was sadly cut out by the farmer the next day to deter people from visiting, and this also was to be a recurring theme in the Pewsey Vale from this year.

WINGED SERPENT SEEDS

Woodborough Hill – 9 June 2012

This formation was cut out the next day   © *Steve Alexander*

Wasaki-Quetzalcoatl:

Many of you wish to know the meaning of the three little wriggling sperm. They are winged serpent seeds. It is my creative power shooting into the land to fertilise the body of dear Gaia. She needs the energy, dear ones, also of you human beings who enter our circles in wonder and joy. Your positive and loving energy unites with what we imprint into the earth to strengthen and glorify our work.

When many people come and walk in our circles and sit or lie down absorbing the energies, the earth also receives what you, dear ones, give to her in your interaction with our loving energies which pulse up out of the land below you. Thus do we work together already. Those who are more conscious among you know this and align their work with us in full awareness, which greatly increases the power. We need you to fully awaken, dear human beings, and call you to work with us now in the formations on the sacred land of Gaia.

Three days later on the 12 June came another crop circle near Silbury Hill, which you can see in the photograph rising in its mysterious pyramidal form out of the landscape beyond the field of wheat. This time it was a little fivefold formation with a lively and graceful movement to it. The central circle was linked by slim curving arcs to each of the five outer circles, which were connected in turn by other fine curved lines to the first arcs, and inside it you could feel the energy dancing lightly from circle to circle.

STARRY DANCE

Silbury Hill - 12 June 2012

Amuna Ra- Star Self:

It is a delightful dance to enliven you human beings, bringing the Pleiadian energy directly down to earth for you to feel. You feel your starry lineage in this formation. It awakens with love all those who come from our stars. And all people feel our joy in the starry movement, and they are transported into the turnings of worlds. They are energised by our love and moving song. The small circles send the resonance of our song to the earth and the lines are lines of direction, of force, pointing the way.

Direction to Future Crop Circles

The 'lines of direction' refers to the cross which appeared as a second phase on 13th June. Crop Circle Connector shows several images taken before the cross arrived in their 2012 archives. In this photo you can just see the cross pointing up past Silbury Hill. In looking back at this while writing the book, I thought at first it might indicate where the circle came the same day crossing to the next field, but I soon found that it didn't.

I spread out the Ordnance Survey map where I had marked the co-ordinates of all the 2012 circles and compared several images of this formation so I could approximate the angle to the tramlines and to Silbury Hill and other features of the landscape. When I had plotted the directions of the cross to the best of my ability, I used a couple of long rulers and a big set square for the right angles and carefully extended the lines of the cross in the four directions.

What resulted filled me with wonder, and really helped orientate me in this sacred and magical landscape:

- The line to the WSW, the left-hand horizontal arm in our photo, points directly as the crow flies to the exact spot on Bishops Cannings Down where the formation was to come six weeks later on 24th July.
- The vertical arm of the cross to the NNW goes right past Silbury Hill to Windmill Hill just where the crop circle would appear on 25th July.
- The right-hand horizontal arm extends to the ENE and indicates the Chalk Pit where the Spiral would arrive in just over seven weeks on 2nd August.
- And the lower vertical arm to the SSE goes right to Woodborough Hill where the great Eye of Quetzalcoatl would come ten weeks later on 20th August.

You can have a look on the map and follow the lines of direction for yourselves.

The paradox doesn't escape me that I was so amazed at experiencing such connections through extending the arms of a cross drawn on a map of the physical topography of the earth. On the one hand I am completely at ease with doing such an exercise on the inner planes in meditation as in the Star Cross Meditation at the end of this book (pp.184-187) but I am not naturally geometrically inclined in my human existence. It takes a lot to get me to pore over a map and draw out lines with accuracy. Even my star being friends tease me about my orientation on the earth, suggesting if I get lost trying to find a crop circle that I would actually appreciate the sat-nav my children encourage me to acquire! (But I still prefer to look at the lie of the land, if I can see that I don't have a problem.) When first following these directives, I hadn't adjusted at all to the probability that in a simultaneous existence 'I', as my Star Being Self, is oriented in several directions, and dimensions all at once.

But I was becoming more and more intrigued by this evolving mystery of connection and alignment and simultaneous time. Here I could see the star beings' awareness of all these 'times' at once – for us on the earth on the 13th June 2012 they hadn't yet happened, the other four crop circles were still in the future. Yet looking back, we see now they were somehow 'there' all at once. Prediction could be seen as drawing from an awareness of a co-existing whole, a nexus of probability, which is not separated by time as we usually reckon it.

The star beings also do not seem to have the same kind of free will as we human beings to alter a situation. We have choice at every stage, and human choice can radically alter a probable future. The star beings seem to focus precisely on what presents itself as most likely in the moment out of the many possible futures. At this point, Peroptimé chipped in with his perspective on my musings:

Peroptimé:

Dearest one, it is true we do not have the same kind of free will as you, that is the prerogative of human beings on the Earth. We do see past and future at the same time as the present, they are all present in - not a continuum for that suggests a linear unfolding – but in a sphere. The phrase 'Sphere of all Possibilities' is good, and in this sphere we can see what is more probable for it is prominent. We see the intentions of beings, where their will is directed, and thus we can activate our will if there is a need to counteract or support the will of others. As we work for the Light, it is obvious that we will be attracted to intervening in actions of dark intent, and encouraging those which work for the Good.

Silbury Hill seen from inside the crop circle.　　　　　　　*© Amuna Ra*

FROM ONE WORLD TO THE NEXT

Silbury Hill - 13 June 2012

The very next day, a lovely little formation formed of five circles arrived stretching from the same field of wheat to the neighbouring barley field.

Amuna Ra-Star Self:

Dearest one, it is a crossing of the threshold from one world to the next. The opening is wide now, and we place our circles of balance just where they are needed, that you human beings may cross when the time is right into the next dimensions. You are called to this point from the Starry Dance, that you may know that it is through movement and resonance that you cross between the worlds. You are wiser in your Star Being than you are yet conscious of in your human life, though we are stretching your consciousness at all stages, dear counterpart.

SOLSTICE FLOWER with GLYPHS

Golden Ball Hill - 20 June 2012

© *Steve Alexander*

Exactly a week later came another graceful flower, this time for the Summer Solstice at Golden Ball Hill across the Vale of Pewsey from Woodborough. In the morning the Star Beings asked me to go there quickly, but when I arrived the farmer was waiting and was not allowing anybody to go in. He told me they were going to try and lift the lay so the wheat would still grow. He said if that didn't work they would destroy it along with the small circle at Huish, also in a field of his. We talked on a while about the crop circles and what the local farmers felt about them in their fields. He told me that while he appreciated the beauty of the circles as art, they had decided the phenomenon was just too much with all the people who flocked to the fields. Then I sat up on Golden Ball Hill in the sunshine and looked down on the delicate curving forms, enjoying conversations with two lovely people from the US who had been able to experience the energy inside earlier. When I was alone I could speak with the star beings through writing in my notebook, and I enquired who had made this circle.

Hot Light Rays Alter the DNA

Wasaki-Quetzalcoatl:

Oh, Amuna Ra, Amuna Ra made it and gave the form to Wasaki, who imprinted it on the field for the Solstice with the hot light rays which bend the corn by altering the DNA within the stems. In this case the lay was light, the stems only lightly altered in order to impress the curving forms onto the field. It is a flower in full bloom on Midsummer Day, connected each petal with the next, as your hearts connect one to the next.

Amuna Ra:

Please tell me the deeper meanings of the form.

Wasaki-Quetzalcoatl:

Oh dear one, it is still strange that you do not know in your human mind what your soul does. The flower formation imprints the joy of blooming into the ground to help Gaia and to help the human beings who live upon her to realise there is great joy in life and to lift their spirits. It is a message of pure joy on the Solstice.

Star Being Signatures

Amuna Ra: What are the two glyphs either side of it?

Wasaki-Quetzalcoatl: They are our signs, our signatures.

Amuna Ra: But neither is yours, is it? (Quetzalcoatl's glyph can be found in the longer section on signature glyphs, p. 193.)

Wasaki-Quetzalcoatl: No, dear one, they refer to the lightships who laid this form into the corn. It was Peroptimé (*I inwardly saw the trident-like glyph*) and Anaximander (*I saw the triangular flag*) who were in command of the craft which made this in the night.

Making Crop Circles

I stayed most of that warm Solstice day sitting up on Golden Ball Hill reflecting on what I had been told. When Wasaki said first that I in my star being 'made' the circle, the impression I received was that 'I' conceived its design, this being part of my star being's task as a Keeper of the Records. I passed the design on through thought transference, telepathy, which is instant and the way we communicate all the time, to Wasaki with whom I work very closely. I have often seen him standing just behind or beside me as I am bending over a complex-looking console of shimmering white light, monitoring the earth and its needs.

When I say 'I' here, I am referring to my parallel or simultaneous existence as a blue Pleiadian star being. She has appeared to my inner sight as a traditional skinny ET-type being with large rounded almond-shaped eyes, about four and a half feet tall, a deep rich damson blue in colour and emanating sheer love. Wasaki in his Star Being is similar but silvery-grey coloured and smooth-skinned, with beautiful loving dark eyes. He is a being of great strength and power, yet has a mercurial and playful demeanour. He it was who first contacted me from the Galactic Federation in 2009 and informed me that he was 'the Commander of the Fleet of the Galactic Federation' and that I had work to do with them and needed to awaken to a consciousness of my star being. Little did I know at that time how this contact would immediately set in motion dramatic changes in my life.

Now I know that he was speaking of the Andromedan Fleet of lightships who presently have as one of their tasks the protecting of these sacred lands of Avebury and the creating of crop circles as 'medicine for the earth' and human beings. To my perception these lightships and craft are formed from light, though light which is slightly denser than purely spiritual light, because it is densified through having a distinct purpose to do with the Earth which necessitates stepping down the frequencies.

The Balls of Light are Star Beings

The small craft are also organic, and can shift their forms as needed, or show themselves according to how a human being can receive them. In other words, some people will see them as more solid looking and more metallic, others will see them as balls of light, and still others experience them as pure moving energy or even as resonance, as sound. So the perceptions of them are affected by the consciousness of the one perceiving, as well as by the beings commanding the craft.

The functioning of the lightships and small craft are controlled by pure thought, which is the same as pure will in the Higher Dimensions. And pure thought-will is instantaneous in its effect. In the case of the crop circles we are speaking of here, the lightship is also the 'body' of the star being who is making the formation, which is why the grammar and the human concept of 'who made it' can become very confusing. For the star beings themselves are the balls of light which so many people have seen moving fast then disappearing in a field. They use the form most appropriate to the task in hand.

The Mysteries of Star Being and Higher Self

With this thought-perception I have finally been able to grasp how it might be possible for 'me' in my star being to create a crop circle out of light. I had the distinct experience of my Higher Self as a sphere of light being incorporated into my subtle bodies on Cherhill the night I saw the City of Light in the stormy skies (see p.23.) I knew it to be not only the Celestial City spoken of by mystics of old, but also the mother ship on which I work over these sacred lands as my Star Self alongside my colleagues from the Star Councils of Light.

I knew also that the reception of my Higher Self marked an initiation in consciousness which encompassed the awareness that my Higher Self was the same as my star being – the two concepts from different human thought systems merged. I know now that there is a consonance of angelic being and star being. Behind the hierarchies of angels, as behind the gods of old, stand the beings from the far-distant stars who have worked to help the evolution of the earth from the very beginnings. And when we are able to let our consciousness rise sufficiently, with an open mind and no preconceptions whatsoever, neither from the commonly held scientific world-view, nor from our favourite spiritual or metaphysical systems, then we can behold the mysteries, and take them into our very being. Then they become part of us, and we become part of them. We are transformed, and we become conscious of existing simultaneously in other dimensions. In other words, we know from our own experience that we are multi-dimensional beings.

WINGED SERPENT or DRAGON

Adam's Grave, Alton Barnes - 25 June 2012

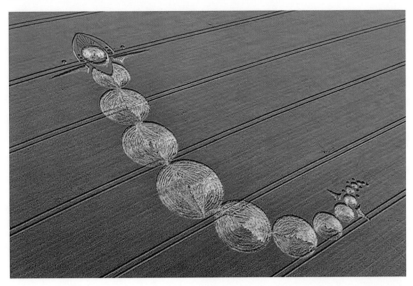

Photos © Steve Alexander

Peroptimé:

Oh dearest one, the winged serpent has grown big and shows himself on the sacred lands where the dragon energy runs fast through the earth. It is to tell you he is here. He has returned and awaits your recognition of his being with you now.

Being cut out the same morning

Cutting the Crop Circles

The farmers in the Pewsey Vale were cutting out many of the crop circles to deter visitors from their lands, and we are fortunate Steve Alexander was flying that morning so we have a record of the forms of this great dragon as they were when they were created. In the bottom picture you can see the tractor working in the tail area, the fine diamond-shaped forms of the lay in the circles have been obliterated and the head is already almost completely gone.

Conversation on Star Being Signatures

Amuna Ra: The big dragon at Adam's Grave shows two small circles above its wings and six along its tail, they feel like balancing forms... or is it a signature?

Peroptimé, for the Star Councils of Light: They are balancing forms, and also your signature, dear one. It is hard for you to conceive of being responsible for these great formations, is it not?

Amuna Ra: Yes, it is very hard. I often forget your words straightaway. Who made the three little winged serpent seeds? I did love them when I first saw them, but I think that is because I love Wasaki and the dragon energy.

Peroptimé: It is, dear one, and it is because they are yours.

Amuna Ra: But there are no circles outside the forms whatsoever.

Peroptimé: No, it is an unsigned work by a shy artist, dear one.

PLEIADIAN CIRCLES

Cherhill - 25 June 2012

A Wondrous and Short-lived Star

On the same day as the Winged Serpent at Adam's Grave there appeared this lovely formation. The centre had two narrow concentric circles around it, and in the centre the woven lay formed an exquisite six-fold star that touched my heart deeply. *(I am standing in this photo, having just arrived.)* I stayed for four hours and many people came and spoke with me, and there were some very special meetings. There was a beautiful high vibration, gentle and still and very clear.

An hour or so after I got there a tour group arrived, their guide ushering them in to the centre announcing loudly that it was well-known the crop circles were all man-made. The whole group sat down right in the centre to have their photo taken, oblivious of the beautiful star they sat upon. Then up they got, and on they went to the next Wiltshire attraction.

The visible beauty of the centre was completely gone, yet the gentle joyous calm energy remained. I sat very still in the same place, along with another beautifully sensitive soul, holding the continuity and keeping a certain inner contact with the star beings.

On-Going Alchemical Process

Others came and went, all honouring and respecting the formation. Some who had been there earlier were deeply shocked to find the centre destroyed so soon. I was experiencing how these creations of utter beauty are totally subject to the consciousness of we human beings as to whether they survive. Yet I also knew that the energetic working into the earth and into human beings is not dependent on the design's longevity, for the interchange had taken place, and we were all still feeling the magic of the on-going alchemical process.

That day I was in a wordless communion in the circle. It was not until I was preparing this book that I asked the star beings to tell me of it. I was feeling its Pleiadian vibration and enquired if 'I, in my star being' had anything to do with it. It was my star being self who answered, rejoicing that I was working on integrating the awareness of my soul into my thinking capacity.

Amuna Ra - Star Self:

Oh dear one, you did! You-I made it for your delight, and it was a delight to you, was it not?

All circular formations ringed around lead human beings out of their three-dimensional perception into the higher dimensions, they begin to receive cosmic energies and open to star messages. Healings and recalibrations are effected and all who enter leave happy, with their energetic frequencies raised. Their vibrations tend to resonate with that of the circle they are in, according to how open they are and how long they remain.

Cherhill after the central star had gone.   *© Steve Alexander*

DRAGON ENERGY

Knoll Down - 26 June 2012

Photos © Amuna Ra

The next day brought another small formation at Knoll Down just along the road to Avebury, composed of five circles all connected and graduating in size to a tail. The photo above was taken in the largest circle and the one opposite is of the lovely swirling movement in the tail. It was the twisting movement of the connected circles that suggested another little dragon wriggling across the corner of the field, this time very simple and unadorned.

The Star Councils of Light:

Oh dearest one, you rejoice in the beauty of the energy of our little dragon. We have to make more as they are often cut out, and we wish to remind you of the serpent forces which course through these sacred lands. They renew your energy as you rest within and absorb our frequencies. You are also subtly recalibrated through receiving the impulses of the dragon energy activated by our starry vibrations. This recalibration adjusts your bodily systems that you may be more receptive to the incoming energies of this special year, and open to the communications that we wish to have with you, each according to your abilities to do so.

We wish to awaken your consciousness to our existence through a direct transmission of energies. This is why it is so important to spend time quietly in our circles. Gradually you will begin to perceive on ever higher levels, and your bodies will become more and more healthy as they take on their optimal functioning through the healing vibrations of our energy, which is particularly strong when the circles are freshly made. We delight in your company, dear human beings. It is we, the Star Councils of Light, who speak with you.

BALL OF LIGHT

Stanton St Bernard - 26 June 2012

On the same day as the little dragon form at Knoll Down this simple circle arrived near the barn below the White Horse. The crop was less mature and pressed down more firmly in a similar herringbone-type lay.

Peroptimé: Oh dear one, it is a depiction of one of our small craft. We use them to fly down into the fields and make the forms in the growing grain for you to find. This shows a ball of light, as you call them, as you may see it from the ground. You may notice the similarity to the orbs which you capture on your cameras, for both phenomena, orbs and balls of light, have a similar origin. We leave this mystery with you so you may solve it. We made the form of our craft so you may know that we will come soon and expect our arrival in the fields. It is to tell you this.

CITY OF LIGHT

Stanton St Bernard - 29 June 2012

Across the road, three days later a spectacular Celestial City with five tall spires topped by a shining star graced the rainy field of green barley. From below the five rectangular areas hung five drops, melodious like heavenly wind-chimes. Out from the sides stretched two thin lines, pointing. At the time I didn't pick up on the hint to follow the direction of the pointers, I was living in the inner experiences of the changing direction of the energy flows.

The Star Councils of Light:

Oh dear one, this is a starry message of direction. The forces flow down from the star into different streams towards the earth. The rectangular blocks are the transformers which step down the codes into the correct form for their earthly destinations. Then the medicines are sent on as drops of light. These drops of light enter into the earth bearing the star forces which can alter the frequencies of the earth so as to help her in the changes she is undergoing.

We show you earth beings these images in the fields so you may begin to understand the way we work into the earth. Even when human beings do not comprehend all layers of our meaning, the picture enters the consciousness of all who see it, and this picture imprints upon your minds our starry codes. Gradually you begin to open to our messages. Better still is to enter the fields whenever possible and as soon as possible, for then you can feel the energy that is impressed through the light into the ground, and you receive our medicine directly into your being. It is medicine for you human beings also and it alters your frequency, just as it adjusts the frequency of the earth your mother.

In a Drop of Light

Peace descending,

Dropping down with the gentle rain,

Green barley swirled

To potentise,

The dose soaks into earth,

Graced to receive

In the rainy times.

The land is still,

Wind stirs in grey skies,

Rain falls,

Only fire is

Quenched

That we may receive

In stillness of

Green.

Opposite © Steve Alexander

The Gifts of the Reversed Flow

In the City of Light the energy flowed in powerful currents, which seemed to be transduced by the transformers. To my surprise when I went in on 3rd of July, I felt the energy currents were distinctly reversed from what the star beings had first described. I felt that they were now flowing up from the drops of light towards the star, as if the medicine had done its work and the earth energy, the serpent power, was now ascending.

On this visit, feeling this reversal of the energy flow strongly affecting me, I spent a long time in the central drop where peace descended and settled all around me, preparing me to move on.

I then walked up into the central transformer where I received a powerful energy activation of the solar plexus centre, an energising of my Sun Chakra.

Finally in the star, came a beautiful, almost ecstatic, enlivening of the higher heart and third eye centres, a receiving of pure cosmic energy.

In the central transformer of the City of Light

© Amuna Ra

The three verses slipped in after each stage of the experience and I wrote them down in my notebook, damp with the rain.

Into the Transformer

Approach

Of raw

Power.

Hidden fire

Ignited.

Solar fusion

In

Steady

Intent.

In Starshine Suspended

In starshine suspended,

Weightless in space,

Receiving a silvery

Delicacy,

Rising from below,

Shimmering,

Permeating,

Easing into the Heart,

Melting,

Filling the Heart

With spreading warmth.

A spinal shiver,

Energy rising,

Reaching the throat,

Broadening smile,

Face dissolving

In interior space vastly expanding,

Receiving blesséd

Star Light.

Earth Healing
and
Star Contact

July

FLOWER OF LIFE

Waden Hill, Avebury –1 July 2012

© Steve Alexander

Appearing on the hillside above the stones of the Beckhampton Avenue, this pretty crop circle attracted large numbers of visitors from all over the world who could easily walk up to it from Avebury. Many would disappear into the little triangular chambers between the petals and sit and meditate unseen in the warm sunshine of early July. Every line in the whole formation was curved.

The Star Councils of Light:

This is the Flower of Life within a softened triangular form. We have made it all with curved lines, to ease the experience of the intake and absorption of our medicine. For when the lines are straight the energy flows fast and direct, and sometimes a gentler ingress is needed, a gentler approach, that it may be received the more easily both by the Earth and by human beings.

ACTIVATING COMMUNICATION

Wanborough Plain - 1 July 2012

This large formation composed of two equilateral triangles within a circle appeared in a wheat field right beside the busy M4 motorway with its constant flow of traffic near Swindon, on the same day as the Flower of Life at Avebury with its curved and receptive triangular forms. In stark contrast the energy here was active and dynamic. Every line in the triangles, one superimposed upon the other, led you by the shortest route, as straight lines do. Except in the curved areas within the broad outer ring where the lay was inviting, you were not inclined to sit down and rest.

Peroptimé for the Star Councils of Light:

Oh dear one, it was made by the Sirian fleet to warm the hearts of all human beings who love the sacred geometry, and can decipher our meanings with ease. There are two intersecting triangles forming a six-pointed star, showing 'As above, so below' which is always represented in this symbol. We wish you all to pay more attention to *your* part in the co-operation between human beings and star beings. We are only able to work with you and through you, to the extent that you clear your own vessel to receive our transmissions.

We will assist you in this clearing work whenever you ask, for we need your willing co-operation with us. Entering this formation in close proximity to one of the arteries of your transport and communications system will suffuse you with the intensified energies which will activate or enhance your capacities to communicate with us and hear our communications with you.

Opposite © Steve Alexander

The narrower lines within the triangles are the lines of force which intensify the transmissions, you are aware of that when you look at the pictures from above, are you not, dear ones?

For these seem to you to come towards you and invite you into the formation. If you remain still and quiet in the epicentre for long enough you will be able to access our messages, and we will be able to take further the re-calibration of your systems to the extent that you have worked on yourself beforehand. When this down-loading is complete you will feel a shifting in the energies.

At that point move to one of the softer curved areas and allow what you have received to settle into you and be absorbed. Rest there in the gentler energies and feel the meaning of our communication.

Eight days after the great circle beside the motorway, another dragon or winged serpent appeared on the green slopes of Picked Hill in the Pewsey Vale, not far from Adam's Grave where the short-lived serpent had been two weeks earlier. This was a big winged serpent, coiled in on itself with its tail over-arching its head and a star at the end of the tail. The head was one big eye once more. The straighter line of the coil in front of its face, or eye, had a strange, almost claustrophobic effect on me – it was just too close for comfort. And later when you compare the relaxed forms of the nesting dragons at Avebury of 1 August, you can feel the difference in dynamic.

THE EYE OF THE WINGED SERPENT

Picked Hill, Wilcot - 9 July 2012

© Steve Alexander

The Star Councils of Light:

This dragon at Picked Hill bears the same formation in the head area as the previous formations which did not remain long, for we wish you to see the eye which watches you. It is the eye of the wingèd serpent, the feathered serpent, who roams these lands as the dragon power in the Earth. For the great Quetzalcoatl is none other than the dragon power which courses so powerfully through these sacred lands.

You experienced the form of his body as being squeezed in, and so it is, squeezed in by the pressure of the accelerating times. You too, dear ones, are often experiencing being squeezed, being pressured, by time are you not? But the power latent in the coils of his body can be very great when unleashed, and you can feel the whiplash potential of the tail.

Quetzalcoatl, a Star Being

We have coded the end of his tail with a star to remind you of your starry origins, as of his also. For the great Quetzalcoatl who returns is a star being. Behind all the ancient gods are beings from the stars who seeded the Earth and brought their wisdom to the evolving humanity. This knowledge now returns to consciousness in many of you. He is here with us and active in making these formations which speak with you and allow you to receive the energetic recalibrations you need in the processes of change you are undergoing along with your dear Earth.

Note the outstretched wings which hold the balance despite the pressing in. We have added the necessary medicine in the two small circles which further assist the balance of the whole. When you are feeling pressured, we ask you to seek the balancing medicines to restore the equilibrium in your souls. Walking in nature and entering our formations to receive the energies into you are ways of re-balancing. We send this new formation to assist you in your awakenings, and in your comprehension of our work through the crop circles.

SUN CIRCLE

Etchilhampton - 12 July 2012

This is such a lovely picture of human harmony - all sitting in a sun-circle, the symbol of unity and cosmic connection, of oneness. The centre is open and free, and there is a great deal of lively unstructured movement in the lay. All the people sitting around the periphery are still, and equal in their diversity.

Peroptimé for the Star Councils of Light:

Dearest one, there is great activity on your sun at this point in time in preparation for the events to come at the Winter Solstice when it enters the Fourth Dimension. You can see the turbulence created by the solar flares as the energy of the sun is released due to the transformations within the sun. Your sun is changing in readiness for the galactic alignment with the Great Central Sun which heralds the passage of your whole solar system into the Fourth Dimension.

Your Earth planet is undergoing similar transformations within her being as she prepares to cross the dimensions just before the sun. You see these changes do not take place mechanically, but organically, and the period between the two crossings is most momentous for you who live upon the Earth.

Peroptimé.

In the last chapter of this book, The Transition to the New Earth, the star beings speak of the transition of the Earth into the Fourth Dimension on 12 December 2012 and the Sun making this shift nine days later on 21 December 2012. They give many pointers as to what this means and in particular how it affects human consciousness.

But back to the summer, on 17 July, nineteen days after the City of Light had first arrived, a new and different circular form was added above the star. Within the circle was a big central star with two smaller stars on either side and further circles and crescents top and bottom, rounded in its grace rather than angular like the spires below. This was followed by a third phase three days later, which added the slender lines in graduated steps extending outwards at 9, 12 and 3 o'clock and the elongated diamond below the lowest drop of light, which then united the extended formation as a whole.

CITY OF LIGHT - MOTHER SHIP

Stanton St Bernard, ph. 3 - 20 July 2012

Peroptimé:

Oh dear one, you know it is the City of Light and you were told how the transformers step down the energy so it may be received. The new giant star matrix is to show the glory of the Mother Ship when she is seen as a ship – from below, so to speak. She is a great circular city, the City of Light, spanning these lands and protecting the sacred sites. It is our power centre. We work from here alongside you in your star body. We monitor the lands of the Earth, and send down our light and energy to recalibrate and balance the Earth and human beings. Our small craft, the spheres of light, fly out from the Mother Ship, as do larger craft when they are needed for more extensive flights. These craft are entirely of energy and light. They are not physical in the sense you on the Earth think of physical, and yet they have a certain physicality as they are a little denser than etheric substance. Matter and spirit are a continuum, and it is sometimes difficult to say where one ends and the other begins.

Amuna Ra: Ah, so both the first phase and the circular addition are different views of the City of Light, which *is* the Mother Ship?

Peroptimé: Yes, exactly, dearest one. The perspective only is different. They can be viewed from any angle.

Amuna Ra: And the narrow lines extending outwards are the flight paths of the smaller craft, the balls of light, aren't they?

Peroptimé: Oh yes, dear one, you see you *can* read our codes now, even in your human body.

Amuna Ra: Only with your help, by tuning into your mind, dear friend. Thank you. Oh, are these also lines of direction to show where the next crop circles will be made?

Peroptimé: Follow the lines on your maps and see, dear one.

Directions to Future Crop Circles

When I got the map out and did this, I was again filled with wonder to find absolutely clear correlations, which you can follow also if you wish and check out my map reading.

- The 9 o'clock direction led straight to the spot where the formation would come at Bishops Cannings Down four days later on 24 July.
- The 3 o'clock pointer indicated past Alton Barnes to Woodborough Hill where the Eye of Quetzalcoatl would come on 20 August.
- And the 12 o'clock line by-passed Avebury to the east, and led right to Hackpen Hill where the 2012 crop circle season would culminate with the two small circles and the huge and impressive Metatron's Cube at the end of August.

Peroptimé:

Dearest one, it is amusing to us to see you still marvelling at what is to you in your star being a normal day's work, so to speak. You will learn to read the codes in our scripts in the corn with much more ease in your human body, and rapidly now that you are becoming so conscious of the codes.

BEING TRANSPORTED

Wanborough Plain, phase 2 - 21 July 12

© Steve Alexander

The metamorphosis of this formation came three weeks after the first phase and shows as the mid-green areas in the photo above. It accentuated the underlying geometry of the star tetrahedron and emphasised the lift-off potential of the grid in the centre. Standing on the centre point, I felt the sheer power of the converging forces and an inexorable thrust upwards, as if I were the rocket being launched. My consciousness then could not quite encompass what happened, but I know I left quite changed. As I write this, I am curious as to what did happen then?

Peroptimé: Oh dear one, you came to visit us in the City of Light, and it was a joy to see you. It is a pity that your human mind cannot yet retain all that you experience. In time your consciousness will expand and you will know the joys of living in consciousness in both our worlds.

Amuna Ra: A friend wonders if Enoch-Metatron could have made the Wanborough Plain crop circle in its two phases of Star of David and Metatron's Cube with curved space-time grid. Did you?

Metatron: Oh dear one, your direct question amuses me. The direct answer is: Of course, I did. There is more to it, though. It was made in conjunction with teams of the Star Councils of Light, those star beings in their craft of light with special responsibility for the crop circle making, whom you know well. Yes, I mean the Andromedan Fleet captained by your dear Wasaki-Quetzalcoatl.

Summer Days

These were the long hot days of the summer holidays, and I sometimes had my grandchildren staying. One of the girls has a strong connection to the star beings and really loved the crop circles. She it was who gleefully spotted the next formation at Bishops Cannings Down on the hillside as we were driving there. Inside, she felt so happy and ran the lengths of the sides of the big square in great excitement. When the star beings spoke with me later about it, they contrasted my Pleiadian origins with hers on the star Lyra. She felt instantly at home in the energy in the formation, whereas I didn't feel particularly akinto the energies in the circle itself, and needed to contemplate the aerial photograph in order to rise in my consciousness into an experience of the facets of planar space glinting off each other in light-filled colours. Thus do the formations call us in different ways according to who we are in our star origins.

PLANAR SPACE

Bishops Cannings Down - 24 July 12

© Steve Alexander

The Star Councils of Light:

Dear one, this great circle that your star child grand-daughter loved, is more for those of her lineage than yours. It was made by the Andromedan Fleet to alert human beings to the squares within squares and the myriad angular relationships of planar space which project you into further dimensions when you allow your consciousness to slant off them. You are seeing now a scintillating array of facets each stretching into infinity which are our means of communication and transportation in inter-stellar space. When you human beings succeed in allowing your consciousness to live in these higher dimensions, as you have just done, thus do you glimpse the reality of their existence through your own experience.

I didn't manage to visit these three little formations at Hinton Parva. In addition to the star being head on the next page, which you can just see in shadow at the top of this picture, there was a circular form, a lightship seen from below, and a series of three circles leading to a fourth with two rings around it equidistant from each other with the inner ring touching the circle.

Hinton Parva – 25 July - the two formations in the field with the star being head in shadow at the top of the picture. © *APS Ltd/WCCSG*

STAR BEING HEAD

Hinton Parva, Fox Hill - 25 July 2012

The Star Councils of Light:

Oh dear Amuna Ra, you wonder if the head was made by us? It was, indeed, made by us, by our Pleiadian teams. It shows a Pleiadian Being like you, but you did not visit it. We called you through this one, and your grand-daughter would have loved it too... Yes, we will tell you more. The series of circles leading to the two rings around the Earth show our fleets coming into the atmosphere of your planet in two stages. We have also shown you one of the lightships of our Pleiadian Fleet which is captained by a Light Being like you.

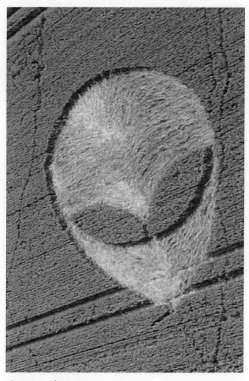

At the time I was still trying to absorb the consciousness of my simultaneous existence as a star being - it was almost more than I could take in - and you can feel the star beings' gently teasing tone here, as they hint that I am intimately connected to this one.

MEDICINE FOR THE EARTH

Windmill Hill, Avebury - 25 July 2012

Peroptimé, for the Star Councils of Light:

This is a message to you human beings to speak of our medicine for the Earth. We inject the right amount of energy through the sixteen circles joining together to take the dose into the ring which receives. The reception of the medicine takes place in the larger central circle and it is absorbed into the Earth at this point. There is some continuation of the momentum out of the ring on the other side until it dies away having done its work.

We are continually monitoring the Earth at her sensitive spots such as near Avebury to ensure that she is on course with the changes she is undergoing. The great solar flares from your sun star are a consequence of the transformations taking place on the sun, and the effects have now reached the Earth.

Recalibration

We needed to recalibrate the energy to balance out the effects of the great energy of the solar flares. You can see from the thin circle how much the Earth was knocked out of her orbit by the strongest of the solar flares. The medicine we injected was to strengthen her and correct the overstepping of the mark, so that the angle of tilt was corrected, and not too much. You human beings have been receiving the effects of the solar flares also, in great boosts to your energetic systems. Sometimes this is so great for sensitive people that you had to be stopped so that you would rest and allow the reception of this energy to settle in your systems properly. Several of our channels underwent

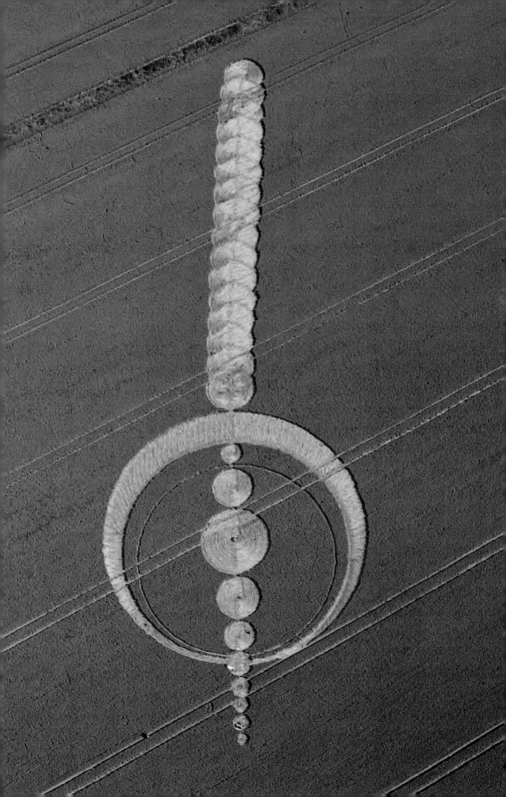

'accidents' to prevent them being too active during this time, for many of you human beings do not rest sufficiently to allow the new energies to settle into you. We would wish that you would always listen to your bodies and rest when needed, and especially when you are having energy downloaded into you to recalibrate your systems. Then we would not need to arrange to have you stopped in such painful ways. For some of you are difficult to stop, you do not take the hint as you say.

Deciphering the Crop Circle Messages

Peroptimé, for the Star Councils of Light:

We wish to say that we rejoice that so many of you are able to decipher our messages, all according to your gifts and talents, then many more perspectives on the layers of meaning are made available to all. *(A reference to the Comments Page on Crop Circle Connector.)* Use the feeling of your hearts, dear ones, to discern which of the multitude of interpretations are valid and which are illusion or the application of preconceived ideas.

The formations of Windmill Hill, Oliver's Castle, Stanton St Bernard, Jubilee Copse, Fox Hill and Allington all tell you of the coming of the star beings to the Earth, as does the great formation of 28 July at Etchilhampton.

Opposite © Steve Alexander

EARTH HEALING

Oliver's Castle, Devizes – 26 July 12

© *Steve Alexander*

Peroptimé, for the Star Councils of Light:

This is also medicine, large doses and small connecting doses. All must be aligned in the right way, and we help assist that that is so. Our formations are corrective and helping to your planet Earth. They transmit the energy of the stars into the Earth, which works like your homeopathic doses to balance the Earth energies. The patterns are designed to carry the healing doses of our medicine. The star beings from Arcturus work with healing, for they are great healers with much cosmic experience.

WORLDS WITHIN WORLDS

Etchilhampton - 28 July 2012

© *Philippe Ullens*

The Star Councils of Light:

The message of our circles within circles is that we wish you all to be aware of the enfolding of the Earth in the loving arms of your star brothers and sisters. The 33 and the 22 are the craft of the Star Nations who come ever closer to your dear planet. The double numbers greatly increase the frequencies available. We have opened a clear pathway, a portal, which you see connecting to the ring of the atmosphere around your Earth and our largest mother ship is poised directly above, along with very many of our smaller craft who are waiting in the wings to enter the atmosphere of the Earth when it is possible to descend and land upon the Earth and reveal ourselves to you.

This great formation is indeed a picture of worlds within worlds, and the advent of our ships which surround your Earth in any case already. We are the 33 and 22 surrounding your dear Earth, coming ever nearer in our smaller craft and entering your atmosphere. We love the planet Earth, for we are your elder brothers and sisters. Many of us have lived upon the Earth, and many of you have lived amongst the stars.

Star People Working with us Already

We are not as different as you might at first assume. We wish to show ourselves en masse to you, show ourselves surrounding the Earth en masse in your skies and landing on your ground. We wish the connecting path between our lightships and your planet to open up as a 'free' way so there may be an easy coming and going between the Earth and our ships. We would like to invite those of your world who are interested in our light technology to come aboard our ships and learn from us.

We have much to share with you that will assist your evolution and make easier your lives. We know that many will react in fear and dread, we know that your governments are plotting to prevent our arrival and stir up the fear of attack. But we also know what you do not know: that we have many thousands of our star people already in key positions in your world's governing bodies. And we know that change will not be as hard as you might assume.

The Portal to the Earth

The centre at Etchilhampton from the portal   © Steve Alexander

Trust us, dear ones, little by little, we are sharing with you, the ones who have dedicated their time to opening to telepathic communication with us, more of the events to come, more of our preparations, and as much of our plans as it is possible to share at this time. Your trust is much needed, dear ones, for then you stand fast, strong and true, and will be the ones who speak of us from your own experience and knowledge. You are our friends and co-workers who will introduce us to those who come later to an awareness of our existence through the shock of our arrival.

Star Beings Wish to Make Contact

Metatron:

The meditations sending the Love in your Hearts for all humankind with the intent for the best possible outcome are having an effect. Do continue, dear ones, to hold the world events in London in your daily meditations and to call on the assistance of the Star Councils of Light, for it helps greatly to ensure that the events predicted for the 4 August in the Manton Drove crop circle take place in as smooth a way as possible.

We would encourage you to speak with as many people as possible about the coming of the craft of the Star Councils of Light, of the coming of the Star Beings openly to make contact with the peoples of Earth and to stabilise the world situation. We will ensure that your ruling bodies are stabilised by the replacement of many of your world leaders with those who work for the light and are dedicated to the wholesome evolution of the Earth. These people are already in place behind the scenes or waiting to step into the positions of power. They have necessarily been veiled before the time was come, both for their own safety, and so that the coming of the Star Nations may take place as planned.

We ask you all who are partially aware of these imminent events to stand firm through the apparent chaos which may at first develop and to trust in our good intent and our ability to stabilise the situation in a relatively short time. We need your steadfastness, your love and trust, in order to reassure the people of the planet Earth that there are those who understand what is happening and who welcome your star brothers and sisters.

For it is true that all Earth people are connected at some time in their past to the stars. We are all family, and there has been much interconnection between the star beings and your planet over the ages past. Now the Earth has reached a critical stage in its evolution, and it is necessary to work together once more the people of Earth and the star beings who have always supported your development.

Re-awakening to our Star Origins

Behind the gods of ancient times stood your star families: in all the great early civilisations of your world like Ancient Egypt and the Mesopotamian cultures, India and China and the Mayans, the Greek and Norse gods, and right through till now in the indigenous peoples of your world who have retained a direct connection to the star people and the spirits of the living world around them. Many, many of you in the so-called civilised parts of your planet have also re-awakened to your star origins and are establishing your own direct connection once more through expanding your conscious mind to encompass these realities and to come into communication with us through channelling.

We call on you all to speak out fearlessly of what you know in your inner beings, to ease the rapid waking up and acceptance of what will shortly take place upon your planet. People will become aware for the first time that UFOs are real space craft, that 'aliens' are your star family, that the star beings come to help the world and offer the priceless gifts of their advanced light technologies. These people will need the help of those who have had longer to come to an understanding of these matters. Your task, dear ones, is to reassure and to help people comprehend what is happening, to tell people that you have been in communication with these star beings for some time, and that their intent is wholly benign, for they wish only to help the peoples of the Earth.

Metatron, 29 July 2012

RE-CONNECTING THE CODES WITHIN

Four Mile Clump, Ogbourne Down - 29 July 12

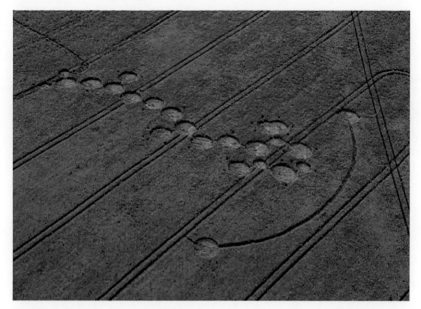

The mysteries within us in a field of poppies   © Philippe Ullens

Many crop circle researchers recognised that the beautiful Four Mile Clump crop circle showed a molecular structure very close to Vitamin A, essential to our functioning in our human bodies. Being an artist I just saw the amazing beauty of all the connecting links in their different relationships yet clearly working together to perform a function. They seemed to me to be snaking across the field from out of the red of the poppies towards the broad bow in the greener parts of. the linseed crop balanced at each end to receive the living elements. I thought it was an echo of the movement of the three little baby dragons snaking over a completely green field earlier in the season.

Amuna Ra, Star Self:

These, our circles in the flowers, show you a little of the mysteries within you, of the chemical structures which unite you with the universe. For you are formed of the same movements and flows and relationships as all life in the universe, the frequency only is different.

Your scientists will begin to understand these processes when they are able to take on board the frequency of vibration. Your artists understand these processes, but cannot describe them for they live best in the realms of feeling.

Connecting us to the Stars

The very molecules within you, all of your cells, all of you, are undergoing vast changes invisibly within. Your DNA blueprint which marks you out as human beings is being activated with the codes that have been long dis-used on your planet.

These codes are codes which connect you to the stars and which, when fully operational, will transform you into the multi-dimensional beings that you are truly are. Your heritage is to transcend your heritage, for that is what becoming fully human means, dear one. It means to rise to the ranks of the divine and take your place amongst the hierarchies. We celebrate the growing divinity of the human race in the fields of flowers.

ONE OF THE POSSIBLE FUTURES

Allington - 29 July 2012

This was also cut out almost immediately   © *Rebekka Schuermans,*
courtesy of CropCircleConnector.com

On the same day as Four Mile Clump came the beautiful clarity of this formation at Allington, which also did not remain beyond the first morning. The channelling about this striking image astounded me as I wrote it down. I could hardly believe what I was hearing and writing. I knew it not to be thoughts of my human mind, yet I could not understand how my Star Self could be saying what she was when she started. Fortunately I did not stop and interrupt the flow, and it began to make more sense once she got to the second paragraph.

Amuna Ra, for the Star Councils of Light:

At Allington you see we have descended right down into your world of the four directions and are united with you in peaceful surrender. All is well, the circle is complete, and we are rejoicing that we have been received as your star brothers and sisters. We are in negotiation with the leading people of your governments to form a new way of working together for peace and prosperity upon your planet. There is an echo of the loving quality of our work immediately above the place where we meet together in the centre.

This is our longed for scenario, one of the possible futures that could come about. It is of course impossible to say whether it will come about or when it will come about, but it is our fervent wish that we may work with the leaders of your world governments to restore peace and prosperity on your planet Earth.

In the words of my Star Self, Amuna Ra, here we can glimpse something of her non-linear consciousness. The star beings easily conceive of different future scenarios co-existing at any one point in our time, and they work wholeheartedly to bring about the 'longed for scenario'. They live absolutely in the moment, and what they say relates only to that. The next moment, if there is a new situation, their orientation changes. Theirs is a vast all-encompassing consciousness, yet in channelled conversations I realise it is not only a matter of us human beings continually stretching our consciousness to comprehend on multi-dimensional levels, but that the star beings also are learning to understand how we human beings function. It is a mutual learning process of adaptation and adjustment, a learning how to co-operate and work together with respect while retaining our independent identities.

PEACE *(in binary code)*

Windmill Hill - 31 July 2012

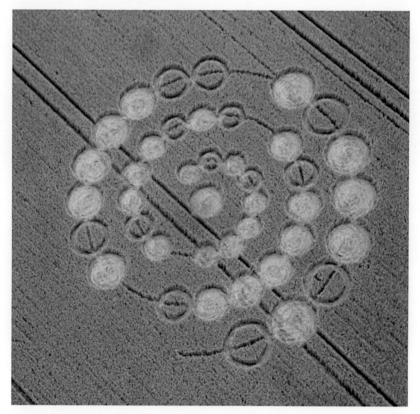

© *Steve Alexander & Monique Klinkenbergh*

Amuna Ra, Star Self:

We come in Peace, dear ones, we wish to work for Peace amongst you and Peace in your Hearts. We showed you the Pipe of Peace last summer (p. 192.) Peace now coils comfortably around the centre and waits, as the serpent-dragons wait for the propitious time.

Waiting for the

Propitious

Time

August

FAMILY OF DRAGONS

Avebury Stone Circle - 1 August 2012

© Philippe Ullens

This dramatic formation of three nested dragons coiled around a broad still centre echoed the circular forms of the Henge. The arcs forming the dragon's backs were graduated in steps like in so many of the 2012 circles and each ended in a shining star, another theme since the City of Light. It was so close to Avebury that lots of visitors who had never seen a crop circle before could easily go in. I spent happy hours in it, with friends and with my grandchildren - finding we could all sit in the baby dragon's smallest circle and be unseen in our little circular house - and at night I spent time alone under the big round harvest moon in peace and stillness.

The Star Councils of Light:

Oh, dearest one, you are with your family in the midst of the family of serpent-dragons, who wait nested together for the propitious time in the sacred lands. The time will come when humanity is ready to accept our overtures of friendship and kinship. We the Star Nations have signed ourselves with the stars in the tails so that you may know of our presence close by with you. We are waiting. We come in peace. We wish to aid you in your awakening to the needs of the Earth and the healing of humanity, for both belong together.

Our Star Selves

We wish to assist you in your reaching for the stars, for your fullest potential as human beings, which is to recognise your own higher being as a star being, one of the divine creative ones. Your home is not truly of the Earth, for long before you chose to begin your earthly incarnations, you existed, dear ones, in spiritual realms, on other star systems. Many of you are becoming conscious of these truths, and sensing your kinship with the starry realms, sensing your homes in the stars.

This does not mean that you abandon the Earth, far from it. For as you begin to see your place on a planet in your solar system, the star system of your Sun amongst other star systems in the universe, so do you truly value and honour the living being of the Earth who sustains your life and you truly value and honour your life upon the Earth.

You know you are part of a whole that is far vaster and far more magnificent than ordinarily realised, and you know that you have a unique role to play as part of this whole. You are also recognising that the energy which you feel in the Earth below your feet, the dragon energy, is the serpent power, the creative power of the Earth as a cosmic being.

Thus can you feel in the three nesting dragons the coiled energy of the serpent power of the Earth, the starry serpent power of the Earth, waiting here at peace. We are coiled around each other and around the Earth, waiting and ever guarding this most sacred place of the heart of this land. We are waiting for the time of transition, for the time of recognition, for the time of awakening – for the propitious time. It is we, the Star Councils of Light, who speak.

The Star Councils of Light, 2 August 2012

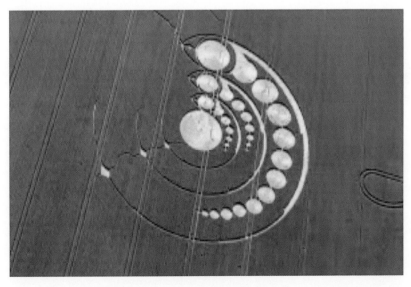

The Avebury dragons with the star beings' signature in their tails.   © Philippe Ullens

TRANSFORMING FEAR

The next afternoon, I sensed the vibration of the Star Councils of Light, and greeted them, knowing they wanted me to take down a message to share publically for them as soon as possible.

The Star Councils of Light:

Oh Amuna Ra, we greet you also, dearest one! We wish to speak of the coming events. We wish to ask you to give out our words as widely as possible.

We wish to alert you all to the need to work on your own fear-based responses, for fear can lurk in the lightest heart.

And sometimes when light-workers resist the facing of their own fear, they deny the existence of the dark altogether as it is so much nicer only to dwell in the Light

We wish you to dwell in the Light, dear ones, but if you have not looked into all the crevices of your hearts and cleared the old baggage, both emotional and outdated mental concepts, then fear can creep in when confronted by the extra-terrestrial realities.

At sunset, going into the 20cm wide spiral at Chalk Pit., p.113 © *Amuna Ra*

111

So in these days, examine yourselves and ask if you are ready to confront the star beings face-to-face. Ask yourself if you are to meet one right now, apparently in your dimension, what would your immediate and truthful reaction be? And many of you will discover that they would react with shock and surprise, and some element of fear, as well as the love and wonder and welcome you would wish to feel.

We say this, dear ones, so you may prepare yourselves sufficiently deeply. For when you become aware of the fear lurking in the depths of your souls, then you shine a bright light upon it, acknowledge and accept it, and in this process it will transform, for the dark cannot exist in the bright light.

Do this work now, dear ones, for all remnants of the old fears must disappear before you are ready to complete the ascension process and before we will be able to show ourselves fully to you.

You can do this today! Do not feel it needs to be a long process. It depends entirely on your ability to face yourself with all honesty, in the truth of your being, just as you are right now.

Know that you are loved in every instant just as you are, and know that we will assist you to complete this process of transformation as soon as you begin it with a real intent to face yourself, and prepare yourself to meet us.

Contact in the Fourth Dimension

It is we, the Star Councils of Light, who speak to you now. Know also, dear ones, that though we may show ourselves apparently in your Third Dimension, it is becoming hard to use these terms as the Earth transcends, for what is apparent will be happening actually in the Fourth Dimension, but visible to all.

For your experience as humanity is rapidly changing, and your abilities are rapidly awakening, even in those who have no concepts of ascension or spiritual development. This is partly due to the ascension process of your Earth planet; to some extent she carries humankind with her. This aspect of the Fourth Dimension may help you understand any anomalies you may notice when we reveal our presence amongst you.

It is still most important that all of you who are on the Path of Light in consciousness do the necessary work to maintain your hearts and minds as clear and receptive as possible right now, so you may perceive the reality accurately.

Good food, and not too much of it, and plenty of water at all times will help you keep your channels clear. And consciously opening your hearts in meditation and prayer to us will assist us in the present moment greatly.

We will speak directly through as many of you as we can. We are most grateful to those channels who have done the arduous work of fitting themselves to receive the high vibrations of our communications. These we recognise as souls who are our co-workers both upon the Earth and in the higher dimensions.

Know that you are loved always and that we hold you in high esteem, oh human beings, as your star brothers and sisters.

The Star Councils of Light,

3 August 2012

Opposite: A perfect spiral of six rounds leading in to a still centre   *© Steve Alexander*

CHALK PIT SPIRAL

Clench Common - 2 August 2012

I went in at sunset on the 4 August, entering by the round chalk pit *(top in the photo overleaf)* and walked the length of the field to the circle which is the ante-room of the spiral. Following the spiral in to the centre, against the flow of the lay, was an arduous and slightly dizzying journey. It felt like walking through stiff bristles. Yet I found it exhilarating, my nerve-ends were tingling and my energy was much enlivened. I spoke with the star beings in the central chamber and received their healing gratefully after a long day working at the computer.

Re-energising in the Spiral

The Star Councils of Light:

Oh dear one, you feel the energy of our circle replacing yours. Drink it in, and absorb the vitalising speckles of light – that is what you felt brushing against you – speckles of light, star-dust, dear one! Absorb the star-dust into your energy field and receive our blessings and our thanks for today's work. We love you, dear little Amuna Ra, being of light, dearest blue being who dances and sings our celestial songs.

Receive in the peace of the evening as the night falls. Now is the time to let go and be re-energised. In the night we will appear and speak with you. You are sleepy now, totally relaxed. We smile to see your human body so relaxed so quickly. You are quick to restore for you have cared for your body in the last years and allowed us to heal you often in our circles. Let us now heal you fully. Lie down, dearest one, and receive the serpent power into you and up through your Stars Within. (*Chakras*)

Orbs: Beings in the Fourth Dimension

As I walked round the spiral out of Chalk Pit, I took this photo of the rising moon - the small bright circle - and noticed afterwards that it was full of orbs. Here is the star beings' response to my telling them of the orbs in the photo:

Sky full of orbs with the full moon at Chalk Pit Spiral on 4 August 2012   © Amuna Ra

The Star Councils of Light:

Oh yes, dearest one, we came! You felt us and heard our words to you, and your camera saw us. You wondered if this was a fourth dimensional occurrence that the camera picked up. It was indeed. The phenomenon of orbs which are not seen but registered on digital cameras is a crossing of the dimensions. Thus much is recorded that is not visually apparent to most.

116

SUN WHEEL OF JOY

Milk Hill – 5 August 2012

© Philippe Ullens

The Star Councils of Light:

Oh, dear one, this is a Sun Wheel of Joy. It recalibrates your energy systems so you may hold more light. All who enter this circle leave lighter, with more light within them in the cells of their bodies. You saw the light dancing around you when you opened your eyes after absorbing the energy you had received. *(Many little points of brilliant light had filled my vision, and I saw everything glistening and shining all around me for quite a while afterwards.)* Your perception was enhanced and you could see and feel in the Fourth Dimension as well as the Third. The Sun Wheel is a portal into the Fourth Dimension and all who enter are changed whether they realise or not... It is good that the farmer permits you all to partake of this cosmic energy bath.

We ask you to connect with us strongly in the next days, dear ones, for we are coming ever closer and wish to be met with love and understanding. Feel us in your hearts and open your inner perception to the subtle changes in the world around you. Know that we love you dearly and wish to assist you in your evolution.

Star Help and Deflection of Threat

On Sunday 5 August 2012 during the Olympic Games, the Northern Line of the Underground in London was closed for several hours. All that was reported was that it was due to 'an electrical fault.' On asking what had happened, I received a response from Metatron describing how the wish of the star beings to show themselves to us was thwarted by the urgent need to stop a bomb threat, and how the meditations for the safekeeping of the Olympics helped the Star Councils of Light helped them to do this successfully.

Metatron:

There was a dispensation changing our plans so that the star beings could not yet appear to your world as they had to divert several attempts to bomb the Olympics. They were successful, and your meditations and fervent prayers helped them to succeed in their task. We do not wish your world to be severely disrupted if at all possible, so it had to be made safe from this recent planned terrorism. You have realised that your Earth, Gaia, is expanding her aura greatly. Now the star beings are completely within the aura of Gaia, they are part of her now. You are all one. Much has taken place over these last few days, and now all human beings are operating partially in fourth dimensionality, along with Gaia.

This is why your sense of time is so disrupted, for there is no time in the Fourth Dimension. It is causing many confusions and maintaining your emotional stability and ensuring your mind is completely open and free at all times is vital now, dear ones, so you may correctly discern what is happening around you. Maintaining your love and trust in the forces of the Light is also indispensable for the wholesome working out of the present scenario. As you say, hang on in there with us, dear Lightworkers.

There is a great deal going on behind the scenes. Continue to hold the world events in London in the Love of your Hearts, and maintain the Peace of your Hearts, knowing that this serenity is the best assistance you can give to the world at this present moment. The exercise of clearing yet more of the old baggage of fear and confusion, and outworn concepts from your minds is a preparation for what you will be undergoing in the next period ahead. We love you dearly and are always available to help you. Only call on us in those quiet moments of your meditations.

Portal into the Fourth Dimension, showing the exquisitely woven lay in the centre of the Sun Wheel, Milk Hill - 5 August 2012   *© Steve Alexander*

Mass Conscious Working with the Star Councils

The call had been put out by several Lightworkers for people to consciously meditate in their hearts for harmony in the Olympics, amongst them was David Eicke^v in the UK. When I decided to do my meditations at the time he suggested I felt a huge presence of souls united in their hearts and wills to help safeguard the Olympics. In a channelled conversation with me later the Master Hilarion spoke of the thousands of people who had meditated to help the Star Councils of Light in their work. I asked him if he meant that literally.

Hilarion:

Oh yes, dear one, I did mean that you galvanised thousands of people into inner action, thousands of people took up meditations to support the Star Councils of Light. It was the greatest conscious working with the Forces of Light for the Good that has taken place so far upon your planet.

This was the decisive factor that swung the balance and enabled the Star Councils of Light to avert the attacks of terrorism that were in the process of being enacted. You are aware that the underground trains stopped running on the afternoon of Sunday 5 August, and you are aware that this was connected with the events which were hushed up in order not to disturb the great festival of the Olympic Games which was in progress.

The Decisive Factor in the Energetic Battle

Without the love and prayers of so very many human beings the star beings could not have been successful. The conscious dedicating of time and love and goodwill was the decisive factor in the energetic battle, along with the consciousness amongst human beings of the role of the Star Councils of Light. For all things take place on an energetic level as well as the physical level, and if the balance is tipped energetically, the outcome on the physical plane is altered.

This is what happened when the strike at the underground trains was prevented. Thus there was no loss of life, nor disruption. But all the forces of the Star Councils of Light had to be mobilised to work for the prevention of the aggression, and thus yet again their hopes of being able to show themselves to you people of the Earth at that time could not be realised. You will see that this is just what the dark forces wish to prevent, and they foster many different ways of diverting the energies of the Star Councils of Light so that they may not come into an open working with the peoples of the Earth. For when they do, there will be no possibility of the dark forces having any influence more upon the direction your world takes.

The Star Beings Need Our Trust

At 2pm on Saturday 11 August, the day before the Olympics ended, I again felt the vibration of the Star Councils of Light very strongly, and asked if they wished to speak. There came this heartfelt plea.

The Star Councils of Light:

Oh Amuna Ra, we do. We wish you to post this message on the websites for all to see and share. Tonight we come close to you as we have said. We wish to show ourselves tomorrow, if the conditions are favourable, and we wish you all to prepare to meet us within your beings. Meditate and pray for our favourable reception and welcome, dear ones, for we need your help. We need the assistance of all Lightworkers on your planet who know of our existence and have pledged themselves to work for the forces of light.

Last weekend we routed the attempts of the dark forces to derail our plans, and now we come once more to the point where we will be able to show ourselves to your leaders and on the world stage. We know that some of you are losing heart when we are not able to come at the time you expected, and we say to you that your trust is much needed, dear ones, for you are unaware of what is taking place behind the scenes. We need your unconditional trust as well as your unconditional love. Trust is a mark of your knowledge and full acceptance that we truly work to assist humanity. Your timescales are not the same as ours, and yet with the opening portals the gaps are narrowing. You will become more used to how time is warping and apparently shrinking. You will become more used to how you need to maintain a flexible and fluid trust in our goodwill and support us unwaveringly in our work, even when you do not see it with your eyes.

Unity Consciousness with the Star Beings

We know that very many of you accept the fact of our constant assistance in your own lives and are grateful for it. Now we need the assistance of your constant trust in us and our work for the best evolution of your planet. The Time is Now, and all must unite in unity consciousness with us. We are now completely within the atmosphere of the Earth, breathing along with Gaia, and we wish to breathe along with you in all consciousness, dear Lightworkers!

Become conscious co-workers with us, by giving us your unconditional trust, dear ones, we pray of you. Your consciousness makes a very big difference to the frequency of the Earth, for every vibration which emanates from you affects the whole. Let your light shine out with pure love and with the trust that all will work out for the good in the best way possible. Then we may be welcomed when we are able to reveal ourselves to your planet Earth. Our gratitude to you, dear ones, in advance for your help.

SHINING CHALICE

Stone Pit Hill, Bishops Cannings - 11 August 12

© *Steve Alexander*

On the 12 August, the last evening of the Olympic Games, I was sitting in this lovely circle of sixteen segments in the evening sun, feeling its peace and shining harmony. A few others were there who knew of the star being' words and there was a quiet inward mood. Suddenly I was called to go home and channel. What came was this clarion call to humanity. I share the message here just as it was posted widely on the internet that evening, for by this point the sharing of these channellings had snowballed and they were being translated into several other languages. You will be able to follow the whole sequence of developments which began with the forewarning of the Polar Clock crop circle on 2 June (p. 39) and see how the devoted love and meditation of human beings was powerful in helping to change the course of events on the weekend of 4-5 August, and led to a very *human* revelation at the end of the Games.

Look to the Skies!

The Star Councils of Light:

Dearest Lightworkers, look to the skies this evening for we wish to show ourselves to you. It may be in an unexpected way for many of you. Remember our words to you in the past days and weeks, and remark the subtle differences in your surroundings.

But look to the skies on this night, dear ones, and you will notice what we show to you. Be aware of your finer feelings, our channel is experiencing a mounting excitement, though she has no thoughts in her mind.

She is full of joy and anticipation of she knows not what. She has not speculated, and has kept herself busy in order not to become too excited. We wish that such an open mind may be more widespread amongst you. We can speak easily through a clear and empty mind, for when we speak it is filled only with our thoughts which are transmitted easily and clearly into words for you to read.

Now, dear ones, to our announcement for you this glorious evening. Look to the skies over the great Olympic Stadium for we wish to partake in your most famous Games. Look to the skies with open minds, and welcoming hearts, for we wish to approach you, dear ones. We wish you to know us now, and co-operate with us for the future of your dear planet.

We wish to share our technological achievements with you to solve many of the pressing problems of your world, and we wish you to work alongside us. We have been very busy behind the scenes clearing the way for this great revelation of our coming, and we wish you to know us on this night.

A Chalice to Receive the Star Beings

There will be many reactions to our disclosure of our presence amongst you Earth beings, and your calmness and steadiness are much needed to reassure those who may at first feel fear. We need your unconditional love and your unconditional trust, we need you to send your Light and your Love to us in welcome.

This forms a shining chalice into which we may descend, and enables our approach to be made easier. Do this for us, dear ones, let the Light of your Love shine out from your hearts in welcome – and look to the skies!

The Star Councils of Light, 12 August 2012.

Athletes assembled in the form of the Union Jack at the closing ceremony of the Olympic Games, London, 12 August 2012   *CC: Philip Pryke*

Further Conversation with the Star Beings

Amuna Ra:

So what did happen last night? I didn't *see* anything in the skies when watching the Olympics, though the gentle skies over my garden afterwards were lovely, the moon exquisite and a couple of orange spheres were keeping watch over these sacred lands. But I was profoundly impressed by seeing all those human beings come together from so many countries of our world when the athletes came in with their faces shining, and I felt such a great love for all humanity and so connected with them all.

Thousands in Harmony at the Olympics

I saw an extraordinary joyous harmony of huge numbers of people choreographed wonderfully and incredibly well synchronised – several big choirs, an orchestra, and thousands and thousands of volunteers as well as professional dancers and reassuringly-ageing pop stars – all in constant movement and flow. And I couldn't help noticing how the crop circle at Stone Pit was a harbinger of the part of the ceremony where hundreds of athletes assembled to form the Union Jack out of their bodies, with shining paths radiating out from the centre. All in all it was an impressive demonstration of how we human beings can work together seamlessly en masse. At one point I thought that this was what it was – the star beings showing themselves as us, *as* humanity. For we are beings of the stars, starseeds all in our origins, and just look at how we can co-operate and work together when we unite our consciousness and intent with one aim.

The Star Councils of Light:

Oh dearest one, we needed you all to realise this, to realise your own power and to start acting on this realisation. It is *your* planet, and you can heal your social structures and governing bodies as soon as you realise your very great power as conscious individuals who *are* spiritual beings, star beings who belong to the whole cosmos.

Realise Your Own Power Humanity

We are working constantly behind the scenes to ease these processes. We need you to notice and celebrate the fact that the changes *are* taking place. Many of us worked with the organising teams for the great festival of the Olympics so you might see the power of humanity, and feel your own strength and courage and determination through the achievements of all involved.

Know that you *are* powerful beyond measure. Open your minds to what is happening all around you and within your dear Earth's aura. Notice the transformations that are taking place right now, as you shift into fourth dimensionality along with your planet.

It may be easier than you think. We wish you to experience what is possible without cataclysms, through joy and harmony, for they are powerful forces of unity. We love you always, dear ones, and wish you to notice the subtle changes all around you. There will be more and more over the next few weeks. Hold us also in the Light of your Love and we will continue to work together with you.

The Star Councils of Light,

13 August 2012

THE EYE OF QUETZALCOATL

Woodbor

.

ough Hill - 20 August 2012

© Monique Klinkenbergh

Nine days later came this exquisite formation at Woodborough Hill, which speaks to our souls on multiple levels and combines numerous themes from this year: crescents, eye, directions with gradations, and Quetzalcoatl's headdress topped by the star.

Quetzalcoatl has Returned

Peroptimé, for the Star Councils of Light:

The complex design signifies in its first layer of meaning the eye of the feathered serpent which has been shown to you in so many of our circles this season. Quetzalcoatl has been watching you ever more closely and is preparing his return. Some of you are very aware of this and he speaks directly within you. For these human souls, he is there with them: he has returned and with them walks the Earth once more. He looks out of their eyes and sees the world as you human beings have made it, for you are creative beings. He speaks within you and sends his messages out to the world through your voices and writings. You work with him and he works through you. It is a wonderful work of co-operation between gods and humankind.

Degrees of Shift of the Polar Axis

When you gaze upon this formation you become aware of the arcs within, with the gesture of their arms reaching out in very specific directions to receive what will be given. Contemplate further, dear ones, what this may mean in an astronomical sense.

The overall formation indicates your principal directions on the Earth plane, and you can both see and feel the degrees of shift of the polar axis as you see the changing alignments along the outstretched arms, in the step-wise shifts. We have sent you these clues in many of our circles of recent times. (cf. The City of Light, phase 3 p. ?)

When you look into the formation from the direction of the inner arc you become aware of the head-dress of Quetzalcoatl, the feathered serpent, overarching you in a protective gesture and waiting for the outer arc to turn so the alignment of forces is complete. The star has descended over his head-dress and his incursion into your realm becomes ever more apparent as he dips down into your reality.

Here you see the two realms are touching and separate no longer, for your Earth is entering the Fourth Dimension and all of you who dwell upon her are experiencing matters beyond the Third Dimension that you are used to. This experiencing of the Fourth Dimension is shifting your consciousness of the realms beyond death on a mass scale. And this is happening for all human beings whether they are aware of it or not.

Spreading awareness

The great task for those who are conscious of these changes is to help spread an awareness of what is taking place widely amongst the peoples of the Earth. Start with those closest to you, and speak in small ways of the shifts taking place and how they affect everyone. You will do a great deal to ease the transition for those you reassure.

If you connect to us, we will help you find the right words for all to receive. Sometimes the smallest gesture of understanding will ease people's travails, and sometimes speaking in depth will be called for. You will know as if by an inner instinct what words to use and when to speak.

Do not hesitate, dear ones, for you are our ambassadors upon the Earth, held in the arms of our love for you. We are with you always, and come ever closer to you.

ENERGY DYNAMICS

Hackpen Hill, 1 - 21 August 2012

© Benjamin Chapman, courtesy CropCircleConnector.com

The channelling below was received in this first small circle at Hackpen Hill while I was there with one of my Star Connecting Courses. It was about 40' across, and more regular on the ground than it appears in the photo. On the exposed north-east side of the hill, there was wind damage to large areas of the field as well as to the circle and I think it was not noticed for several days. However it was well worth going in to experience the dynamics of the energy flow which were dramatic. We moved round the circle sensing the changes in the flow of the energy as we slowly circled round.

You can also look at the photo and do this in your consciousness. Start with the outer circle in the rectangular space bottom left in the picture, and imagine yourself slowly walking clockwise round in the direction of the lay. It takes quite a long time to complete the circle until you arrive back at your starting point, but it is a smooth journey. Now, cross to the inner circle, let your consciousness stand before the beginning of the inner circle *(left half of the image)* and slowly let it move round, again clockwise with the lay, imagining your energy body expanding gradually as the arc widens until you are abruptly stopped and forced to concentrate your energy into a narrower stream in order to pass into the right-hand half *(in the picture.)* You then experience a more powerful focus within as you move onwards, and when you eventually reach the open space you started from, you experience it quite anew because your perception has been transformed through the concentration of your energy.

Learning to Concentrate Your Power

Peroptimé, for the Star Councils of Light:

This circle has been here since early last week. It is our circle in the corn and you are welcome into it. This circle shows the expansion and contraction needed as the Earth transitions into the Fourth Dimension. Sometimes you need to allow your energy to expand and sometimes to contract. You will acquire the necessary skills in both directions. The changes you human beings are undergoing require a fluid ability to regulate your subtle bodies according to the prevailing conditions.

It is no longer only a matter of expanding into the Light. You need to acquire the ability to contract at will and concentrate your power into a focus like a laser beam. With this great concentration of power can you create, and share our work with us. You need to be able to draw in your Light into the centre of your being, not always radiating it outwards, only when it is appropriate.

We are glad you have found this circle as few have as yet. And we ask you to study the dynamics of the changing dimensions, how suddenly an expansion is drawn in and flows on as a concentrated energy. Feel the power of the flow: where is it stronger? where is it weaker? Teach these things, dear one, in your courses, much may be learned through experiencing the dynamics of flow inwardly, in regard to how to regulate your own energy and its flow. This is needed in daily life in order to have the focus of power needed to withstand the pressures of contraction and turbulence in the transitioning ahead. Out of the concentrated energy and focus will come great clarity and perseverance. These are qualities greatly needed.

Teachings on Signature Glyphs

Amuna Ra: Peroptimé, whose signature is the cross beside this circle *(top right of image)*, if it is a signature?

Peroptimé: Oh dear Amuna Ra, it is a signature. It is the signature of Amuna Ra. You teach yourself of the flow of energy. Go back and find this cross and sit in it and channel. You can also further research the flows of energy when you are alone.

Amuna Ra: Dear Peroptimé, was the simple circle with the two rings at Hackpen Hill mine also? It felt like it. The energy was like mine.

Peroptimé: It was indeed, my dear Amuna Ra, you made both the first circles at Hackpen Hill. All who enter the simple circle can feel your joyful loving energy and be at peace.

ONE OF OUR SMALL LIGHTSHIPS

Wansdyke - 21 August 2012

Peroptimé :

Wansdyke was one of ours too, a representation of one of our small lightships, the craft we use to transport us to make the circles and return us to the mothership where we work and live. You recognised the small triangular enclosures in the Metatron's Cube *(which arrived*

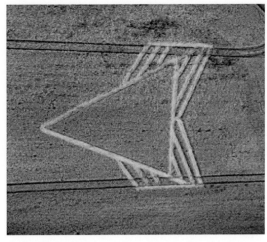

© APS Ltd/WCCSG

five days later) as our small Andromedan craft too. We are showing ourselves to you all, so you become familiar with our ways.

You saw our craft when you lay under the moon and looked to the skies. *(In Chalk Pit Spiral.)* Twice did you see our spheres of light moving fast as they returned to base and disappeared from view.

The formation of four lights you see so often in the skies are lights on our mothership overhead that alert the returning craft to the portals for re-entry. We are always with you. We love you always, dearest star sister.

(Sometimes I see one of these lights flashing like a wink, or changing colour from orange to white, and know it means just this, that they are always with me.)

STILL CIRCLES

Hackpen Hill, 2 - 21 August 2012

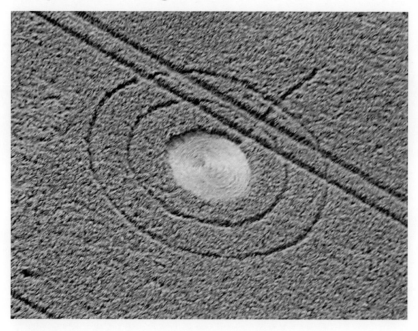

© *Lucy Pringle*

A crop circle of beautiful simplicity was reported on the 21 August in wheat that was nearly ripe. It did not have the straight line you see in this photo, which was an addition that had arrived by 22 August. The energy was soft and gentle and still, most harmonious and healing. I was in this circle on both days, and spotted the new line on the second day. It pointed over the hill just to the left of the clump of trees above the White Horse at Hackpen that you can see in the aerial photograph on p. 138. It was a very clear directive to where the next magnificent formation was to appear in the big field below the White Horse four days later on 26 August.

METATRON'S CUBE

Hackpen Hill, 3 - 26 August 2012

The end of August and early September was a busy time for me with workshops and courses and I was later than usual with posting channelling about this wonderful and complex formation, which everyone referred to as Metatron's Cube. I was prompted by someone emailing me to ask what the Star Councils of Light had to say about it, as she hadn't been able to find anything on the website. She had been told it was Arcturian. I had felt an Andromedan connection, and it turned out to be a joint venture from several of the Star Nations.

Peroptimé, for the Star Councils of Light:

Dearest Amuna Ra, we wished you to ask about this formation and therefore are responding with joy and alacrity, which means all speed. *(It was as if he jumped in with great eagerness, explaining as I was wondering exactly what alacrity meant.)*

This great formation which was the last serious crop circle of the 2012 season, was made by the Star Councils of Light, and we are composed of many Star Nations, principally the Andromedans, Sirians, Pleiadians and Arcturians. Some crop circles are made by the fleet of one specific Star Nation sending down their small craft from the mothership, such as the two small Pleiadian circles which you know preceded this last one.

This one was a composite effort between the Andromedan, Sirian and Arcturian fleets, that it may encompass the sacred geometry beloved of those in tune with the Sirian vibrations, and the etheric launching pad which you discovered in the centre of the three lines of force, which is

Overleaf © Steve Alexander

a point created by we Andromedans to assist those human beings who are capable of ascending right now *(i.e. inwardly rising into higher consciousness)* to experience the higher dimensions. The healing fields of the beautiful interlaced areas around the hexagon were created by our Arcturian friends and you experienced the effects on your energy bodies, as did the dear soul who wrote to you.

Reconnecting the Codes Within

We work together in harmony in this way to serve the Earth and you human beings, so you may be recharged, and healed, and assisted in your endeavours to reach the starry planes and communicate with us. We await your reaching out to us, dear ones, and you will be assisted by our frequencies in our formations when you enter them and allow the energies to work into you and awaken your dormant circuits. You will also receive great benefit from contemplating the design of the formations in the photographs, so long as you do not become lost in your own mental processes.

Feel what happens within your bodies: first your physical body and your etheric body – you feel a desire to stay awhile, do you not? And when you sit or lie down *(or gaze at the picture)* and give it time, your etheric body and your life forces are quickened and revitalised. Your emotional body is stilled and you feel the peace of your heart spreading throughout your systems, which allows the process of reconnecting the codes to be taken further in you. Your mental processes slow down - and eventually stop - and in the spaces between the thoughts, you perceive what is there from a free space and wonder at the glory. Your spirit is uplifted and you feel you can soar to the stars.

Let Yourself Soar to the Stars

We say unto you, dear ones, allow this to happen in you. For we would delight in a visit from you and will welcome you with open arms as we welcome our dear Amuna Ra when she comes to see us.

It is I, Peroptimé, who speaks for the Star Councils of Light and I call on all who receive this message in their hearts to begin the process of making contact with us. Speak with Amuna Ra further about these processes, she will be pleased to hear from you, dear ones.

We send our Blessings of Light to you all in these times of great changes. For all is fluid now as the Earth transitions into the Fourth Dimension, and those who have the courage to grasp the initiative and come to see us will be much rewarded, for there is great work to do together, dear ones, and you are much needed.

Triangular enclosures and woven lay, Hackpen - 26 Aug 2012   *©Steve Alexander*

The Transition

to

the New Earth

WINDMILL HILL, 2

Avebury - 14 October 2012

In 2012 we received the gift of an unprecedentedly late crop circle at Windmill Hill near Avebury. It was in a small field of barley and beautiful wild-flowers, just below the path up to the burial mounds at Windmill Hill, which the farmer had kept as a nature conservation area. Drops of rain glistened on the flower seeds and the beards of barley, and the energy was fine and strong and clear over the whole field. Since the field is left uncut for the wildlife, at the time of writing this book *(Spring 2013)* the last Avebury crop circle of 2012 is still there. Its graceful forms and warm feminine energies were able to work their magic into the Earth undisturbed throughout the great time of transformation in the winter of 2012 to 2013.

Transition into the Fourth Dimension

The Star Councils of Light, part 1:

We do wish to send a message to all humanity at this momentous time through this formation. We are delighted that some crops are still standing this late in the year to conserve the flowers and natural life, and to allow us to send our messages directly to you through our latest circle. The message of this formation is concerned with the impending ascension of the Earth into the Fourth Dimension on the twelfth of December 2012, your triple twelve date (12-12-12). This transitioning over the threshold from the Third Dimension to the Fourth does not mean, as some say to divert you, that the Third Dimension will cease to exist. Far from it, the Third Dimension belongs to the Earth, the planet which supports your life.

Conscious in Two Worlds at Once

What this transition means is that the Earth will now be operating - for she is of course a sentient being with consciousness, as you are, dear ones – also in the Fourth Dimension, the astral dimension, which many of you think of as the astral plane. The Third and Fourth Dimensions will begin to consciously co-exist for the Earth, and as potential for all life that lives upon her.

You human beings journey to the astral plane, every night when you pass into the state of sleep. It is the closest spiritual plane to your familiar 3D reality, it is the realm of dreams and all fluid possibilities. It is the realm first visited after death in order to work through the tangles remaining from your Earthly sojourns. And it is the realm of the stars as the word astral indicates.

The Star Beings Within the Earth's Aura

We mentioned once before in these messages in the summer that the Earth was expanding her aura to encompass the Fourth Dimension and as she breathed out into this expanded consciousness, we star beings and our mother ships and smaller craft, who are present to assist these processes on the Earth, have been enfolded by her within her aura. So we are now truly working alongside you, dear human beings, to help the right unfolding of the Light expansion of your planet and all life which dwells upon and within her.

If you look at the picture of the formation from the air, you see the small circle at the very centre, the heart – the concentrated heart-core of Gaia - and you see her expanded aura in the greater concentric circle implied by the largest thin lines encompassing the five inner circles. This is where her aura is at present, extending and radiating far further out than it did before August of this year.

Opposite: Windmill Hill, 2- 14 October 201 © Philippe Ullens

Greater Ease of Communication

And within this shining aura of the Earth is our activity, ours and yours – for the work of all well-intentioned human beings who seek to understand the messages in the corn and the evolution of the Earth and the cosmos extends now as potential into this astral realm around the Earth.

This is why your communication networks have expanded so exponentially in recent years, and it is why your non-electronic communication networks have also greatly accelerated. We refer here to your spiritual faculties for communicating with each other and with us non-physical star beings (spiritual beings) who operate in the etheric and astral realms in relation to your Earth to assist in the processes of ascension which are taking place now.

Ascension in Consciousness

We are not in accord with those who suggest that you will all be leaving the Earth when you ascend, rather we say that it is an ascension in consciousness which is becoming rapidly available to humanity over the coming period. And we say here that it is a period of many years, not only the remaining months before the Solstice of 2012.

For those of you who have prepared their physical vehicles to hold the light available to you now can rise on the planes and ascend in your consciousness right now, can you not, dear ones? And it is useful still to have a physical body which connects you with all the joys of the Earth plane.

Energy Flow of the Seven Circles

In our formation at Windmill Hill you can observe and feel how the heart-centre is connected in a curving flow to both the enlarged circles above and below it. You can regard the alignment of the seven circles as the energy centres of the Earth, in fluid dynamic, with a focus at present on the third and fifth centres on either side of the heart. See the loving embrace from the heart around both the centres of the sun-power *(solar plexus chakra below the heart in the centre)* and of communication *(throat chakra, above the heart).*

Great power is emanating from your Sun Star at present, and being received by the Earth your mother. This will assist her in her birthing process, and the birth is now imminent, dear ones. Can you feel the flow of the sun-power down towards the root in the great embrace downwards? And can you feel the flow of loving communication upwards in the embrace of the crown, the cosmic opening? Right at this cosmic moment the Earth's inner sight is protected as she focusses on the work of balancing, and it is likewise not yet quite time for the birthing.

We would like to continue this message in a second discourse later which will deal how this formation speaks to the individual human being.

The Star Councils of Light, October 2012

WINDMILL HILL

Avebury - 14 October 2012

© *Philippe Ullens*

The Star Councils of Light, part 2:

Dearest ones, we wish to continue our discourse about our late formation in the field of flowers on the sacred lands of Avebury. We wish to relate how the ascension of the Earth into the Fourth Dimension is affecting human beings. Just as you human beings continue to exist in the Third Dimension when you are asleep and dreaming in the Fourth Dimension – your bodies are still lying in bed, are they not, while you are flying free in your dreams and experiencing the fluidity of the Fourth Dimension or astral plane?

Sphere of New Possibilities

So too will the physical body of your dear Earth planet still exist in the Third Dimension while she is also freely experiencing the fluidity of the Fourth Dimension and the possibilities of extended consciousness that the astral plane brings. As the Earth moves fully into this state of consciousness on the 12 December 2012, so too does all life upon the Earth move with her into this sphere of greatly extended possibilities.

For individual human beings just how they will experience these new possibilities of consciousness will depend on how open they are, on how much they have developed their spiritual consciousness and prepared themselves to be able to receive the vastly increased potentiality of spiritual and star contact that becomes available to them.

Experience of the Shifts

For those who are still relatively asleep, the shifts will seem unnerving and unsettling. They may experience disorientation in time and dislocation in space. The affairs of the world around them may well seem to change in ways hitherto impossible, and this may initially cause great fear and tension. At the same time, there will not appear to be any great problem with these transformations which will take place. Hence confusions between expectations and actual experience will be rife.

This is why those human beings who have prepared themselves for these shifts with greater consciousness, who will welcome the changes taking place, have a great task to spread warmth and understanding around them, to reassure with compassion those who experience initial fear. There is an especial role for those who can understand something of the tasks of we star beings in aiding the Earth in this particular point in your development. We need you to familiarise yourselves as much as possible with our messages of support, with our descriptions of our work for and with the Earth, so that you yourselves can welcome us with open hearts when we come to assist, and so that you can also begin to communicate with us directly. This is much easier than most of you think, dear ones.

Love is the Vehicle of Communication

Within your hearts you can communicate directly with the spirit, with loved ones who have passed from the earthly Third Dimension into the Fourth after death, and very many of you have experienced this for yourself. The vehicle of this communication is Love. It is the Love in your Hearts which transmits your feeling and carries it to the loved one.

You experience this kind of telepathy with loved ones still upon the Earth also, of course. And as your Heart expands and is refined of confusing emotions, as it becomes a clear lake of peace in which your consciousness can rest, then do you achieve the needed stillness within and you will hear our whispers too, the whispers of the spirit and of the star beings.

Star Connecting and Ascension Processes

We have asked our dear Amuna Ra to teach how to ease human beings into this connecting with us in the Star Connecting Courses as she has an easy ability to pass from her clear heart into the realms of the stars and spirit. This was gained through the processes of refining the inner centres that you call chakras, and we refer to as the Stars Within, until they are clear and mobile and operating as two-way portals of reception and transmission. These are the ascension processes and involve great changes to the DNA through the reconnecting of the codes within and the recalibration of the nerve-endings and synapses in the brain and other organs of the physical body. As you each go through these processes, for they are now coming about to some extent in the ordinary course of life as you live on a planet making these shifts, you will experience that the needs of your body change.

Air is Sweeter

We would urge you, dear ones, to pay heed to what your body needs for its nourishment now. It will require food with life in it, freshly prepared, and plenty of fresh water with no synthetic chemicals in it. It will require contact with the life forces of the Earth your Mother, every day, outside in the fresh air. And as you walk the Earth, slow down, dear ones, and notice how the atmosphere, the very air you breathe, is changing now.

The air is sweeter is it not? The shifts are very subtle, and call on you to open your senses and refine your perception. Smell and taste the air you breathe, beloved ones, and give thanks to the Earth your mother that she carries you with her as she is rebirthed into the new dimension. You live in the most precious times, dear ones. For those who are already awake to these processes the transformations will be rapid, and we would call on you to refine your own operating systems within, that you may each be a worthy transmitter and receiver between the realms of the stars and the Earth.

Feeling the Wonder of the Transition

Then you will be able to assist your fellow human beings in the times to come to make the transition into higher consciousness with much greater ease. Then you will be able to ease the fears of those less conscious, that they may open to the wonder at what is really taking place all around you. We will continue these messages through Amuna Ra as the days advance towards the 12-12-12 when we have asked her to hold a gathering in the Avebury Stones, at the Stone of the Heart, when we will come to communicate with you. It is I, Peroptimé, who speaks for the Star Councils of Light.

Peroptimé, 25 October 2012

MEDITATION FOR THE NEW EARTH

Approach the coming times with joy, for all is changing upon your planet, all is being made new. These are times to let your hearts sing out and rejoice, beloved ones, for you are entering the Fourth Dimension along with your Planet Earth, and very many of you will have easy access also to the Fifth Dimension, the realm of Harmony and Love. Walk outside and touch the Earth, for then will your fears be transformed into joy, for you cannot be anything but full of joy when you enter into the Earth's rejoicing at her rebirth. Go with your Mother and rejoice in the New Earth that has been born at this time.

And gather together to celebrate this glorious new beginning. Take the time not only to give thanks to the Earth your Mother, but to gaze in wonder at the new that is born. Open your hearts and extend your senses and allow the new creation to speak to you. Feel the qualities of the New Earth. Breathe in her essence... Take it into your being and be filled with glory, for you are made anew in these times, dear ones...

Notice how you are transformed... Notice how others are transformed... Notice the birds and the animals, how how they are transformed... Notice the stones and the crystals, how they are transformed... Sink your consciousness right down into the Earth your Mother below your feet, and notice how she is transformed... Extend your consciousness into the realms within the Earth, and notice how they are transformed... Feel the beings who dwell within the Earth, and notice how they are transformed...

Send the Love of your Hearts to your Mother the Earth... Send the Love of your Hearts to all beings who dwell within her... Send the Love of your Hearts to the stones and the crystals... Send the Love of your Hearts to the plants and the trees... Send the Love of your Hearts to the birds and the animals... Send the Love of your Hearts to yourselves ... and to all those with you today in celebration ...

And see how you all shine with this Love you send out... See how you all shine in your Lightbodies... Feel the radiance shining out from you...

Melchisedek,

6 December 2012

THE 12-12-12 CEREMONY AND THE 2012 WINTER SOLSTICE AT AVEBURY

The Henge at Avebury © *Philippe Ullens*

As requested by Melchisedek and the star beings, our Ceremonies for the twelfth day of the twelfth month of the twelfth year of this new millennium and for the Solstice took place at Avebury in front of the Heart Stone. Which can just be seen in the top right quadrant of the picture directly to the right of the tree in the middle. People gathered in a circle, and listened to the deep tones of my big Chau Gong reverberating out into the stones and down into the earth. Everyone circled slowly round, sensing the changes in the earth below their feet and in the air all around on that cold and crispy-white winter day, all the while hearing the resonance of the gong sounding from the various points around the circle.

I spoke of the sacred lands around Avebury and the dragon energy of the earth, of the mystery of the crop circles like the Dragon Family coiled in the next field and the beautiful spiral at Chalk Pit. We listened to the hush in the air at 12 minutes past 12, the moment of the earth's transition into the Fourth Dimension. Then I became aware that other beings wanted me to speak their words so they could be known to be present with us in the Ceremony.

Melchisedek and the Star Beings

Melchisedek spoke through my channelling of the glory of this birthing of the earth into the next dimension on the 12-12-12, of how our Mother Earth had taken all human beings with her, along with all life that lives upon her, and of the preciousness of the coming nine days leading up to the 21st December. This is when the Sun would move into the Fourth Dimension at the point of the great alignment of our solar system with the centre of our Milky Way Galaxy, which marked the turning of the ages.

And then Peroptimé directly addressed the gathering on behalf of the Star Councils of Light and spoke of their work making the crop circles from the mother ship, the City of Light above the sacred lands of Avebury, and of their great wish for their assistance for the earth to be received favourably by us. They trusted we human beings would open to their presence as we become more familiar with them and begin to be able to read the starry scripts in their crop circle messages, and that we would call them in our hearts and begin to work with them. He closed by reminding us that they are always 'only a thought away'.

Spiralling In to the Light & Out to the World

We then all linked hands and I led the circle in walking anti-clockwise the three and a half spirals in to the candle at the centre. Each person in turn inwardly released something they no longer needed to the light, before turning round and beginning to circle out again, hands still joined. The moving coils of the spiral passed each other on the way, some still going in and some going out, smiling as we passed for we were feeling our lightness as we spiralled out.

And the great surprise was that when we had spiralled out to the full extent of the original circle again we were no longer looking in to the centre, but were facing outwards to the world. We were all still holding hands, yet each individual commanded a direction that radiated outwards and onwards. Standing like that, we connected in our hearts with all those others the world over who were celebrating the earth's transition in consciousness. And finally we turned once more to face in to our own circle within the stones of Avebury – with a new perception of our connections, and of ourselves, ready now to step into what was to come.

Moonrise at Avebury   *CC: Pam Brophy*

The Galactic Centre and the Solstice

Nine days later came the culmination at the Solstice in Avebury. After joining the huge celebrations in the Henge in the morning when hundreds of people lined the embankments like ancient sentinels, holding the space while another great ring celebrated in the Sun Circle, our Solstice Ceremony took place in the afternoon again at the Heart Stone. We marked the transition of our Sun into the Fourth Dimension on the day of the galactic alignment with a gong meditation, more spiralling and channelling, and linking to the others celebrating the transition of the 2012 Solstice the world over.

The Centre of the Milky Way Galaxy   *PD-USGov: NASA*

Intense activity close to the centre of our galaxy is revealed in this spectacular composite image of 2009. The galactic core is the white area on the right. Photographs taken using infra-red light and x-ray light were combined to show through the clouds of dust that normally obscure the view from the Earth.

21 DECEMBER 2012 – ALL IS MADE NEW

The Highest Vibrations of Light

Sirius Ra, for the Star Councils of Light:

Dear Amuna Ra, I wish to give you a message for the 21st December, the Winter Solstice in your hemisphere. You have nearly completed the nine days between the 12-12-12 and the Solstice. The Earth has passed into the Fourth Dimension and carried all life upon her with her in her transition. You now approach the time when your Father Sun passes fully into the Fourth Dimension as the galactic alignments are synchronised, and the Light he sends down to you is intensified with the highest vibrations of light.

This will take place on the Solstice, at the time when your day is shortest, and after this transition when the days begin at first imperceptibly to get longer, as the Light grows outwardly in your world, so will your experience of the Light grow inwardly, at first perhaps imperceptibly, and then more and more obviously. Note what changes in you and around you as your frequency becomes more capable of carrying Light, as your vibrations rise.

Follow your Heart

Pay attention, dear ones, to the changes within you, to what you long for, to the feelings of your heart. It will tell you what is right for you and you will not doubt it, for you will know that your heart speaks true. And when you know, follow your heart, dear ones, and do what is right for you. Have the courage to allow your lives to change and expand. Do not be hemmed in by the old, it is no longer relevant to you. Allow your consciousness to expand and feel the new perimeters of your experience far beyond what has been possible up till now.

Stretch out your senses and explore the new territory, the new spiritual territory that opens up before you. Let your inner sight unfold, for you all will see far more clearly in the New Age which opens before you. And look at the inner realities of what is before you. Did you not previously discern the consequences of acting in that manner? Before it was as if a veil was drawn between you and the reality of your actions. You did not see how they affected others. Now all becomes clear and you cannot hide or remain hidden. All is transparent and it is impossible to lie and dissemble, for you can be seen, dear ones, just as you are.

Personal Transformation

And just as you are is just as you should be right now. It is vital to accept yourselves just as you are, to face yourselves in all honesty, and to speak your truth with clarity and kindness. For speaking the truth will help others find the way to accept themselves, for before anyone can decide to change, they must first accept just how they are. Seeing with clarity how you are gives the instant possibility of allowing yourself to grow and transform, to grow into a greater version of yourself, a clearer and more honest version of yourself. And this is always for the good, dear ones, always for the good.

These processes will take place with great speed. Much will be discarded in the processes of emotional refinement, of astral purification. For you will not need your old ways any longer in the new times that are unfolding. If you seek to hold on to them, they will drag you down into the morass, and you will feel more and more uncomfortable, more and more as if dug into a pit you have made yourself. And then you have to find the way to climb out once more.

For there is really no choice, dear ones, the new frequencies of light will not allow the old dense ways of being to exist for they are not compatible with the light vibrations. The process is quicker and easier if you allow it to unfold with grace rather than fight against it with all the defences in your possession. Also, dear ones, we would say to you do not repress your feelings. What is in your heart as an honest reaction to a situation needs to be expressed even if it is an expression of anger. Sometimes such anger is justified and has a salutary effect.

Many of you strive always to be loving and kind, for you have loving and kind hearts, and then it is sometimes so that you do not allow yourselves to express what may be deemed negative emotions. These are then denied and repressed and prevent you from allowing your life to unfold as it then becomes a falsehood. Better by far is an honest expression of feeling even if it takes the form of anger. For once feeling is expressed, it moves on and transforms, and the situation does not become stuck.

The life of feeling is fluid and always changing. Feelings are like the waters of the earth, sometimes turbulent and forceful and sweeping all in their wake, sometimes flowing placidly and resting in deep pools, ever moving, ever changing, bringing life. You are entering now a period of great fluidity on your planet when there will be many unexpected changes both in the world around you and in your inner lives.

You are Transformed

Have courage to greet the new, dear ones, to embrace it and move with it, and then your path will open out to the joy before you. For you enter into a time of great joy, a time of greatly increased possibility for joy. Let it enter your lives and your hearts. Let yourselves live and experience the new. It is simply a matter of opening your hearts and acceptance of what is there. You are transformed as easily as that. And when *you* are transformed, your *world* is transformed. And all is made new.

Sirius Ra, 19 December 2012

LIVING IN MORE THAN ONE DIMENSION

In the first few months of 2013 after the shift into the Fourth Dimension I channelled a series of gentle and poetic messages which give guidance on the processes of adjusting to the new energies and to the opportunities offered us by living in more than one dimension. This phase of adjusting and transformation will go on for many more years while we become accustomed to the new energies, and begin to rise to the challenge of how to live in peace on our planet, taking responsibility for our lives and how we live together, and recognising ourselves as multi-dimensional beings.

We are first urged to free ourselves from as much baggage as possible both mentally and emotionally, so we are clear and can use our will unimpeded. As we come into our full power as sovereign beings we will shine in our own light This is a prerequisite for working consciously with the star beings. They will then be able to share with us their advanced light technologies, and we ourselves will find the ways to resolve the problems of our world, especially in the realm of free energy. And, recognising ourselves as sovereign beings, we will no longer have a problem in recognising each other as sovereign beings and being able to co-operate to bring about peace and plenty in the world.

But the challenge of the moment is mastering ourselves so that we are free to use our human strengths for the good of all, and so that ultimately we are fit to take our places as creator beings alongside the other Star Nations in the Galactic Federation. As always the star beings speak to us with deep love and understanding, offering us their constant support in this process, as older brothers and sisters in our star family - if we wish to accept their help. For the choice is always ours, they leave us quite free in accord with the cosmic law of non-interference. But all we have to do in order to receive their assistance is simply to ask. It is up to us.

Releasing Inner Pressure

The Star Councils of Light:

Oh Amuna Ra, hear thou my words! It is I, Peroptimé, who speaks on this day. I wish you to take down a message from the Star Councils of Light for all who would wish to receive it. Ask that the dear friends share it widely with their friends so it may reach many more people who need to hear these words.

Many of you are going through the most difficult times in these early days of the New Year, of the New Earth. For all that remains of the old has to be cast aside and released. But how can it be cast aside and released without being experienced, dear ones? Very many of you have been experiencing great inner turmoil. Some of you are nearing the point where you will not be prepared to undergo this any longer. At this point, it will mean your will is activated, for there are many amongst you who find it hard to activate your will without experiencing great pressure from the inside or from the outside.

It is as if there is a torrential flow of flood water rushing through your soul, which is impeded by the dammed up areas, the blockages, which restrict the movement of the waters within you. This flood water must find a way out, and it will do so by means of the weakest point in your structure, be that physical or emotional or mental. It will burst through for that is of the nature of flood water. It will fill you till it reaches its level and then sit there until you do something about it, until you activate your will for change. And what you must change, dear ones, is yourself. The structure which must be freed, and cleared and cleansed is yourself. There are rescue services which can help you in the gravest emergencies, but bottom line the only person who can ensure the work is done to clear up the flood waters and the damage caused to the structure is yourself.

River in Flood   *River isis CC: Jonathan Billinger*

The Stars Within – Our Link to Free Energy

What do we mean, dear ones, by the structure which is damaged by the flood water carrying the obstructions along with it? We are speaking here of your souls, dear ones, of your subtle bodies, which need to be healthy and functioning in harmony in order that you may live your lives in peace and comfort and productivity. You are well aware, most of you, of your inner chakra system, which we like to refer to as the stars within. These energy centres link you quite literally with the cosmos through their function as connectors of your energy fields with the universal energy suffusing the cosmos, and suffusing you, dear ones, as you live and move and have your being within this universal energy, within the Cosmic All. This is the fount of all energy, the source of all energy, and it is entirely free energy, dear ones, entirely free, totally benign, and totally loving.

As Above, So Below

For love is the creative force of the cosmos, the powerhouse of the cosmos, the powerhouse of the macrocosm. Most of you are familiar with the ancient hermetic principle, 'As above, so below' And you will appreciate that what is true of the macrocosm is also true of the microcosm – and the microcosm is you yourself, dearest human being, do not forget this! You are the structure, the organism, which reflects the divine creation of the cosmos, the divine love of the cosmos.

And the powerhouse of the cosmos, the creative force of love, is your powerhouse also. How can we understand this, dear ones? For it is clear that this principle of universal love is not meant in the sense of human sexual love or love for your family and friends, which is but a pale reflection of it, but is the life force of creation itself which impulses the unfolding evolution of the whole cosmos, including your planet Earth, and the lives of all human beings living upon the Earth. So there is little point in seeking your salvation in human forms of love.

Look Within, with Honesty

Through facing your demons and releasing your baggage, you can free the obstructions to the flow of cosmic energy within you, and begin to align yourself with your life's purpose, with your cosmic purpose. This requires a degree of honesty with yourself beyond that to which any of you have ever gone. For if you had, you would not be experiencing any tension or discomfort in any aspect of your life, all would be smooth and full of joy, a state of constant bliss and connectedness. The first step on the path is always the honest acknowledgement of what you find when you look within. Inherent in this acknowledgement is acceptance, and this conscious acceptance is what allows you to release. For we do feel it is necessary to know what you are letting go of, else you are not exercising your full humanity as a conscious being, and unacknowledged elements can lurk within awaiting their opportunity to surface.

So, dear ones, if your obstruction is on emotional levels, you must allow yourselves to fully feel the feelings, and when you do fully feel the feelings within, then release and transformation will follow on as the dawn after the darkest hour.

If the blockage is in your mental processes, in the habits of thought you have acquired from family, education or your chosen environment, then you need to choose to open your life of thought in such a way that you can begin to exercise the freedom to observe what is actually there and form appropriate thoughts for yourself.

If your troubles have been pressed down into the physical and are manifesting in ailments of the body then healing will also involve tackling the underlying causes in your emotional and mental lives. With most of you, there is work to be done on all levels for the subtle bodies interpenetrate each other as well as the physical body, so an imbalance in one area throws out the harmony of the whole.

Step One: Balance of Soul

This is why all paths of spiritual development in all Mystery Schools begin with exercises to balance and harmonise the soul. We feel that these soul exercises should be seen as an accompaniment to all spiritual training, for as you ascend on the great spirals of initiation you come again and again to ever finer tests and trials. And even as you reach the higher levels there is the possibility of being knocked off the path by the hidden obstacles in your life of soul, as many Lightworkers are experiencing to their consternation at the moment.

You are living at a time of unprecedented changes in the planet you live upon. The Earth has now entered the Fourth Dimension, which means that you also now have the possibility of a rapidly opening consciousness on the level of the spiritual world bordering on the old familiar 3D reality. You are living simultaneously in two dimensions at least, 3D and 4D. Many of you will also have far easier access to the fifth dimension and beyond. But all life on Earth is now experiencing the opening to the next spiritual dimension, which we refer to as the Fourth Dimension. This is bringing you a more transparent awareness of your inner lives, of your dream lives, and of spiritual experience in general.

Learn How to Handle the New Forces

Many of you will be experiencing distinct spiritual connections to those with whom you have soul connections for the first time, both on the Earth and in spirit, and may be feeling overwhelmed or thrown by these unfamiliar sensations. We urge you to take these changes seriously and to seek out those who are more familiar with the new spiritual processes. It may be that it is time to take a course which will help you become conscious of the new possibilities before you, which will help you learn to handle the new forces surging in towards you.

For if you do not exercise your free will in learning to handle these strong incoming spiritual forces and the changes within you, you may find that you are affected and influenced by them to an unnerving degree. For all is fluid in this new time, and when you try to keep going on the old path, however well it served you once, you find that it is now full of potholes and subject to sudden torrents of water pushing debris before it.

You cannot avoid being swept along into the New Earth, dear ones, and you are all experiencing the churning of the waters within you as you are washed clean and the way is cleared for the new energies. Will you go willingly and embrace the transformations as they come to you? Do not expect to know what they may be, for all of you it will be quite new.

As Below, So Above

Open with joy in your hearts, and notice what is changing in the world around you right now. Are there not little green shoots appearing here and there out of the dark earth? We say unto you, 'As below, so above.' When there is new growth from the Earth, and in the hearts of human beings, so too is there new growth in the cosmos, for all of life is interconnected, and each one of you is essential for the whole. Embrace the new energies and you embrace the new cosmos, and in embracing the new, you are utterly transformed. Our blessings upon you, dear brave and courageous human souls, only call upon us to assist you and we will come to your call with our Love inexhaustible. We are only a thought away.

Peroptimé, for the Star Councils of Light,

9 January 2013

New shoots appearing   *CC: Dave Spicer*

LIGHT INCREASING

The Star Councils of Light:

Dearest ones, we greet you from the stars! We call upon you to heed our words as you undergo the transformations currently taking place within each and every one of you. You will have noticed that this period of time when you are slowly waking from the sleep of winter in the Northern Hemisphere of your world is bringing a gradual increase in the available light, not only in the lengthening days but in your inner worlds also. For many it is as if you are awakening from a dream which had captivated you, and ensnared you on a level of your feeling life, your emotional life, or your life of thoughts.

Suddenly it is as if a new day has dawned and you see more clearly: 'No, that is not what I want, that is not what I intended!' And you begin to pick up the threads of your own life path without it being mixed in with the tapestry of another who has chosen to go a different way. And this is all to the good, dear ones. As the threads which make up the life paths of each one of you gradually disentangle, you are each left in the glory of your own light.

Turn that light inwards and see what it reveals to you. Shine the light into your own soul instead of casting it out to illumine another. And when you shine your light into your own soul, you see the perfection, the glory, of just who you are in your own right. You see the glory, the perfection, of your own life path.

And it touches your heart, does it not, dear ones? You had almost forgotten how wonderful is the path you are treading, the path you have outlined for yourself long before your birth into your present incarnation upon the earth. You were caught up in the ideas of others, concepts which had come towards you as you sought to understand the meaning of the times you live in.

2012 - Expectations

The year of 2012 posed many a riddle for many of you. What was it that was ending? What was it that was beginning anew? What are the powerful new energies that are available to you now in this new year of the 13, beyond the 12?

Many of you were filled with expectations, expectations of what might come to pass on a world-scale or a cosmic scale, and many felt a profound disappointment when what they expected did not come to pass and things around them in their world remained much as they had been.

And many of you had inner expectations on the feeling levels of the soul, expectations of this or the other person fulfilling aspects of your dreams, even dreams you were not fully conscious of having. These personal expectations have also in general terms not been fulfilled. What does this mean, dear ones, to experience such disappointment and confusion? How can this be understood in terms of the new energies of this year of 2013?

Your Consciousness is the 13th Element

Your year of 2013 brings you to the unity within the whole. Twelve is the cosmic completeness. One is the individual. You are experiencing yourself most clearly as a conscious individual right now. You are waking from the cosmic dream of wholeness to the awareness that while this is true and undeniable it is not the whole story.

For in addition to the holistic nature of the cosmos as a wonderful hologram encompassing all that is, there is the great power of the individual consciousness, the thirteenth element. And without this power of the individual consciousness you would be quite unaware of the whole, would you not, dear ones?

And herein lies the paradox. Each and every one of you is an aspect of the divine, and you are graced with this experience from time to time, perhaps when you behold the glories of the sunset, or look out on the vastness of the ocean, or gaze into your lover's eyes, or hold a little child in your arms. In these peak moments you touch into the divine nature of all creation, of all souls, of all human being, and you know deep within that, as well as that which you behold, *you* also are divine.

And to be a spark of the divine living in a human body upon the planet earth is a grace indeed, dear ones, for it gives you a freedom to be conscious and creative in your own development which few beings in the universes possess to the degree you have it upon the earth. You are the thirteenth element added to the twelve. The cosmic dance takes place around the centre point which is your individualised consciousness. For you perceive everything from this centre point, do you not?

You are a Powerful Creative Being

You look out upon the world around you from this point of consciousness. You perceive the feelings of those around you from this point of consciousness. You set your intentions and decide what to do from this point of consciousness. You create your reality from this point of consciousness. You are a most powerful creative being, essential to the whole of the cosmos, for it revolves around you, does it not?

And when you begin to comprehend your value to the whole of the cosmos, you begin to value yourself. You begin to perceive the glory of a soul living within a human body, the glory that you are. And from this perspective when you turn your attention to the problems your life has presented you with, you see very clearly that part of the choice you have made in your path of development is to see what no longer serves you in your life and simply to let it go.

For refining your personality self so it may serve you as best it may is a great part of the path of human life. And when you view your tasks from a cosmic perspective it suddenly seems easier to do what must be done to enable the transformation to take place on a microcosmic level with an ease and a grace that gives you energy. For releasing the old patterns always gives energy.

Consider for a moment what happened within you when you realised recently that something was no longer right for you - a thought, an expectation, a connection, whatever it was. Yes, you experienced a surge of joy, a lightening, for you had put down a burden that you realised you did not need to carry. It was not even really yours.

Hidden Treasure

And you experience this increase in the light within as clarity and a simple joy in existence. This is the energetic state in which many of you are finding yourself at present, dear ones, a state of being new born from out of illusion, of having newly opened your eyes and realised you have learned much about yourself, much that was hidden deep down within you. Take a new look, dear ones, at what surfaced in you from the depths during this last period.

 First it appeared as a dull stone, heavy and uninteresting, something to be shrugged off as quickly as possible. But if you pause and take a little care of it, dust it down and polish it a bit, you will uncover the treasure within the stone. Polish it until it shines in all its glory, in its true colours. Be brave, crack it open, if need be, and let its facets be revealed to you. Would you ever have thought that with a little love and care and attention such a treasure would have come from out of the depths?

Overleaf: Solar glory at Crib Goch   CC: Mike Peel

The Key to this Lifetime

Nurture this jewel from within you, for it will be the key to your whole path in this incarnation, if only you take the time and trouble to see it in its entirety. For there is always the danger of dismissing your tribulations too quickly, feeling so anxious to release them and sort them out, only to have the shock of their resurfacing at a later stage still needing to be transmuted, because in reality they were only banished once more to the underworld.

Take care of this precious jewel that you have discovered in your hearts, dear ones, nurture it well, and watch how the beautiful crystal grows. Look inside, into its facets and see what they reveal to your inner vision, for you will grow greatly in self-knowledge out of the trials of this time.

And how is it possible for so many of you to be experiencing the re-birthing of yourselves in this time? It is because you are the children of your Mother Earth, and you have accompanied her through her re-birthing in the period between the 12-12-12 and the Solstice and have entered the Fourth Dimension along with her. All of you are affected by this transition of the earth, and much around you will be more transparent than before.

And very many of you have entered the Fourth Dimension with your eyes wide open, and you are seeing the reality of the illusions you were previously caught up in. For to live consciously in the Fourth Dimension is to be able to steer your own path through the dream-like consciousness of the astral realms, to take up the rudder of your own ship and set it to take you where you wish to go.

Steering Through the Fourth Dimension

No longer will you drift and be carried along by the will of others, for you will feel this will being exerted, or see the energy being sent out, and you will hear the thoughts of others and not be taken in by outer appearances.

Trust every perception, dearest ones, for the inner reality speaks to you in subtle ways. If you feel uncomfortable, ask yourself what it is that you do not feel comfortable with, and you will know and learn from it.

If you feel intrusions into your energy field, know that you can remove yourself from the path of these energies by removing your attention, and that you can work to make your energy field impermeable to all but goodness and love.

If you hear thoughts which are not compatible with your energy, you have the choice whether to continue with these people who choose a different path. Simply leave them to it, for you may not ask another to change, and move on yourself to what *is* compatible with you and to those with whom you can travel further with ease.

The River of Life

This is the river of life, dearest ones, ever flowing onwards, and now you have your head above the waters, and can see sufficiently well to steer your ship with confidence because you trust in your new ability to perceive what was previously hidden behind the veil. You will rapidly become used to your enhanced abilities, and learn to act upon every perception with an easy grace, speaking your truth with tact and immediately to avoid confusion.

And your passage down the river will become a floating in joy as you realise that the river has broadened, that the surface is calm, and it is taking you just where you need to go. As this begins to become your experience, lift your heads and look around you to notice who is there floating alongside and what is beckoning to you, for many of you will be receiving quite new tasks in the near future.

This is something which is always a marker of trials well passed. There are new openings, new work, new associations, and new vistas ahead. Go forward with joy when the new approaches you.

And look up to the stars, for we wish also to work with you when you are ready to hear our call. We are ever there to receive you and welcome you into our realms. Just open your hearts and minds and speak with us, and we will hear you and respond.

You are in our thoughts always, dear ones. We admire your courage as you progress down the river of life with greater and greater consciousness, and we offer you our assistance whenever you wish. Call on us in your hearts, for we are only a thought away.

Peroptimé, for the Star Councils of Light, 4 February 2013

The River Flows On   *CC: River Wensum*

LIVING IN THE FOURTH DIMENSION

A Meditation to Experience the Fourth Dimension

Metatron:

Dearest ones, tune into your breathing and let yourself feel the ebb and flow of the breath in your bodies... Follow your breathing as it slows and deepens and you will reach a relaxed alpha state very soon...

From this beautifully relaxed and comfortable state of being you will be able to enter the Fourth Dimension in full consciousness, and feel it all around you... ... for you live and move and have your being in both the Third and Fourth Dimensions at this time. It is only your habitual thoughts which make you expect things to be as they used to be in the world around you, only your habitual thoughts, dear ones...

Heed our words here, for when you are able to free your thought life and empty your mind, you will perceive what it is like in the Fourth Dimension... where there is no time as you experience it in the Third Dimension, which operates with logical linear time and three dimensional space... There is no time, only an eternal present moment... Everything is in the present moment, the now...

There is no space as you habitually conceive of space between things creating distance, for example... You only have to think of somewhere else in order to be there in your consciousness. It is instant, no time needed and no distance to travel.

Try it now, dear ones, think of a beautiful and distant place that you have fond memories of.... Focus your mind upon this far-off place and imagine it strongly... See the colours ... feel the textures ... hear the sounds all around you ... and smell the distinctive scents of this place...

In your consciousness, dear ones, you are fully there, are you not? Watch and see what changes in the scene before you, when you let it move and unfold in your imagination...Is this not a real experience in your consciousness? And is your consciousness not real for you, dear ones? It is of course real for you...

For some it is even more real than the exterior world. For all of you, when you do an exercise such as this, you experience the power of your consciousness and the validity of your imagination. This is the way it is in the Fourth Dimension, which is often termed the World of Imagination, the Imaginal World. It contains both images and magic.

The images in your consciousness, willed into being by your intention and focus come to life magically and move of their own accord. If you ask a question of the scene before you, perhaps wondering how it develops, you will instantly experience the development.

Try it, dear ones, return to that same scene you viewed a moment ago, and ask either what developed out of it, or what caused it to come about, what went before. Let your curiosity lead you in your questions, for you must desire to know the answer. Ask and you will know, you will know the answer to your question, it will be unmistakeably before your inner vision...

The Power of Focus and a Pure Heart and Will

All depends on the power of your focus, and the intensity of your desire to know. You are a creative being, and in the malleable fluid substance of this realm of the Fourth Dimension, the World of Imagination, all will move and reform according to your desire and what you will, what you intend in your deepest motivation. This is why all the Mystery Schools train their students in purifying their emotional bodies and their wills.

And those who have already done this work upon themselves and prepared themselves to be a fit instrument to move through the astral worlds of the Fourth Dimension will do so with ease, and little confusion at all. To them, the realities behind the appearances will be revealed, for there is no longer a veil between the worlds. They have trained their lives of thought so as to be in command of their own thoughts and refined their emotional lives, so that they know themselves so well that they recognise what originates within their own consciousness and what intrudes from the consciousness of another being. Thus can they instantly determine what belongs to them and what belongs to another.

This strength is most needed to navigate the Fourth Dimension with ease, for when it is lacking then the consciousness is buffeted like being in a bad dream, where the most unpredictable things can occur without your having any control over it. This is not a desirable state of affairs, for it leaves you cast adrift on the astral waves and unable to steer in any direction. It can be a most unnerving experience.

Fortunately, dear ones, there are those who have trodden this path before you and trained themselves to be able to withstand what may come against them and to control and transmute it to their will, that is, their will for the greatest good of all, for none achieve these heights unless they have dedicated their personal will to the greatest good. These are the Way Showers and Teachers of the Path, and you may recognise them by their steadfastness and kindliness and by the love in their hearts. Yet are these heights the aim of all humankind: the goal of being human is to rise to your highest potential, that of becoming a co-creator alongside the angelic hierarchies and the star beings, of recognising that you are a divine creator being in the core of your own self. To reach this goal you will need to realise that you have the capacity to transform yourself, simply by taking the decision to do so, and taking one step after the other, and keeping on going forward.

Selfless Calls are Always Answered

When you put out the call to the universe for assistance in this process of spiritual transformation in a truly selfless manner, you are heard and the response always comes. Though some may not at first recognise the response, for it can come in the form of a trial. It can seem as if you have been deserted by the spiritual forces, even by your own guides, when the test is to stand on your own feet and act out of your own perceptions. For how can you ever rise to your fullest potential if you are unable to act without a higher authority?

You must become truly sovereign, sovereign over your own self. *You* command your will, and do only what you have decided to do, rather than being influenced by those around you, or subliminally by the television and the internet. *You* command your thoughts and decide what you will think about, rather than letting thoughts tumble unbidden through your mind in a ceaseless chatter. And *you* command your life of feeling, rather than being taken out of yourself as you are when filled with emotion, which means 'moving out of yourself,' does it not? Real feeling is quieter and deeper than the surface emotions.

Building the Capacity for Mastery

You may ask how is it possible to do these things? You can train yourself in each area through a series of simple exercises, such as are given in all traditional spiritual paths. And just as when you are learning to play a musical instrument, you start with simple notes and exercises to gain mastery over your body and train it to do your will and become a competent musician, so can you start to train your life of thoughts, your will and your feeling life through a series of exercises which systematically build the capacity for mastery over yourself.

Then you may become a competent creator being who can be relied upon to create what is intended for the Highest Good and not run amok with chaotic creations because the practice was never put in to achieve a real competence. This was always important in all spiritual systems in the past, it is vital that it is taken with all seriousness now by all who wish to become true Lightworkers.

The Responsibility Not to Cause Chaos

For now that you are working simultaneously in the Third and Fourth Dimensions, you need to be able to control your feelings and thoughts and will, so that you do not inadvertently create chaos because of your wild responses to situations, or indeed do real damage in the astral worlds. For a creator being is powerful indeed, and the substance of the Fourth Dimension responds with lightning speed to the will and feeling of the beings who have access to these realms. Have you realised the responsibility before you, dear Lightworkers? Many of you have taken this on board, and have accepted the necessity of cleaning their own house before acting outwardly. These souls are willingly working on what is left of their un-worked-through baggage, and releasing it, and they are assisted at all times as soon as they recognise the urgent need to do this work upon themselves. When baggage is let go of and the burden put down, then energy is released in great quantities that was previously trapped in the old issues. This energy is what carries you forward with alacrity, dear ones, into the New Earth. New meetings will yield much fruit. You will begin to find those you can work with without hiding who you are or feeling you don't fit in.

Shine in Your Own Light

For it is essential to shine in your own light and be who you are, this new being who is being revealed, who does not need to hang back in fear, for in the New Earth all have their place, all are needed to contribute just what they have to bring, just how they are. And this process is speeding up, dear ones, carrying you all with it in its inexorable flow towards the Light.

So when you go with the flow, and show you are willing to learn to play your own instrument to its most beautiful potential, then you will receive all the assistance you need to accomplish this in the shortest time possible. And did we not speak earlier about how linear time is non-existent in the Fourth Dimension? This means that when you commit yourself to this path of purification and preparing yourself to be a creator being for the Highest Good, it can happen in Fourth Dimensional reality, as if in a twinkling of the eye in the old 3D world.

What is all important is your willingness to transmute all that is within you that is no longer needed. It will become harder and harder to hold onto anything which is unfitted for the higher dimensions, and easier and easier to shed what burdens you.

All that is required is the genuine desire to do so. For your wish is your command, dearest ones. Take this most seriously.

Metatron, 15 February 2013

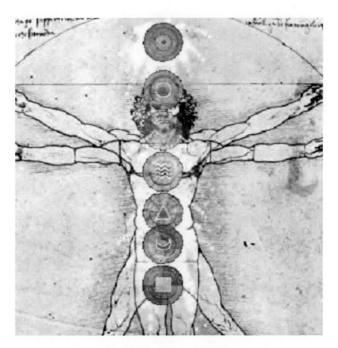

The Stars Within shine from Leonardo's ideal human   PD: Wm.Vroman

KNOW YOU ARE SOVEREIGN COSMIC BEINGS

While Metatron gave this message for the spring equinox of 2013, the first year of the New Earth after the great transitions of 2012, the guidance contained within it for taking stock at the points of balance that the equinoxes offer us each year will apply for a long time to come. For the phase ahead of adjusting to the transformations and opportunities of the New Earth is an on-going process of learning to live as multi-dimensional beings and taking responsibility for our lives on an individual and collective scale.

Metatron:

Dearest ones, with this Equinox when the hours of the light are equal to the hours of the darkness in your world, when all is poised in balance, greet the dawning of the new day and examine yourself to see if you have achieved a similar equipoise.

But do not examine yourself from too deep within, for many of you still have something of a tendency to be too self-critical. Lift yourselves out a little and look at yourself from this perspective, as if you were someone who knows you quite well – as indeed you are!

Using the Forces of Balance to Take Stock

It is a still window, this point of balance, from which you can view the seeds you planted around the time of the last Equinox which have lain deep within all through the long winter and are now growing, all according to how you have nurtured them in this time of inner transformation.

If you have treated them with tenderness and respect they will be growing freely and putting out fresh green leaves, just waiting, some of the early ones, for the first rays of warmer sun to burst into bloom. Others are more deep rooted and grow more slowly, yet they too are stirring, roots spreading and showing the first pink-tinged buds of new growth, are they not?

Look at the Seeds you Planted

Deep down below the life forces in the earth are wakening and rising to meet the forces of wind and water and warmth which nurture their growth. And the forces of all the elements are needed, dear ones, for healthy growth within you also. Look at the seeds you planted and notice if the soil you entrusted them to was right for them.

What you see growing now may well have been watered by tears, and stirred into movement by gales and storms, but we trust you will also have warmed them with the love of your hearts, for they are your children, born of you.

In this window of stillness and balance, take the time to be the conscientious gardener of the seeds you have planted. Yes, we know that many of you will cry out that you love the wildness of nature just as she is and that you do not want to interfere with her perfection.

And yet, dear ones, you will see that even the ancient landscapes bear the traces of man from long ages past. The ancient terraces around the long barrows and hill forts were painstakingly carved out by human beings. Yes, it was done with a reverence and deep connection to the living earth which have allowed them to become so easily part of her by your time, yet they are not simply 'natural'.

Forming Your Inner Landscape

Be conscious of this, dear ones. It is not wrong to exercise your right to take control of your lives, to form the inner landscape as continually the outer is formed. You can do this also with reverence and connection to the living being that is you, and you can do this with the simplest of tools. So be the conscientious gardener and look at the seeds you planted then.

Did you allow them all to grow just as they appeared, or did you remove some to allow others to flourish? Look and see what your inner gardening style has been, did you prune everything in sight and move on to the next task, or did you leave it all to its own devices and slip on the mulch of leaves as you walked?

In your inner gardens clearing space and thinning out dense tangled growth can help to allow the light in, so long as you can recognise which plants you wish to cultivate. You have been doing much of this work in the past half year, and you will now be feeling the lighter for it.

And how have you changed since the Solstice, dear ones, in this quarter year of having entered the Fourth Dimension with all its fast-moving possibilities? Very much has changed within you in this time, has it not?

Actually you are quite different now from the being you were when the earth first came into alignment with the great centre of your galaxy at that time. Notice *how* you have changed. What was it that freed you to take up the new task or calling that you have just begun?

The Glory of the Thread that is Yours to Weave

This taking stock is most important when the forces of your yearly cycles stand in balance at the time of Equinox. For what you will bring to consciousness is an insight into what has been one of the deepest obstacles to your growth in this lifetime. You encounter blocks in your life's path at certain points in cosmic time which, when surmounted, liberate you from an inability to be truly independent and self-sufficient.

This independence and self-sufficiency is the sovereignty you need, dear ones, to realise your mission on the earth at this point in time. And the time of balance of the Equinox is vital for observing how you have changed. Notice the transformation and celebrate the new you! For if you do not celebrate it and share the news, you may yet fall back into the old ways, for the grooves of habit have an odd attraction simply out of familiarity. So speak of how you are different and the fount of new energy that has been released.

Hear yourself sharing your insights with others, and believe what you hear. Pause long enough at this point of equilibrium to let it sink right down into you, till you fully accept the new being that you have become. This taking the time to integrate a full awareness of just how much you have changed is most vital, dear ones, for the healthy unfolding of the next phase ahead.

For we need you to recognise your fullness as a sovereign cosmic being without whom the unfolding tapestry would be missing the glory of the thread which is yours alone to weave.

It is I, Metatron, who speaks.   *19 March 2013*

Bright stars in a neighbouring galaxy   *CC: ESA/Hubble, NASA, D. A. Gouliermis*

THE STAR CROSS MEDITATION

to Connect to the Earth and the Stars
in the Peace of the Heart

Take a long slow breath in and know that you are inspired as you do so. Slowly breathe out and know that the inspiration reaches all as it is set free on the out-breath... Breathe like this three times, or as long as you need till your focus is clear and you begin to feel the Peace of your Hearts... ...

And then centred in your hearts, feel the great stream of white light flowing from high above, through your crown, down through your heart and your root chakra and right down below your feet deep into the earth below, uniting you with all that is above and all that is below... ...

Now feel a second horizontal stream of white light streaming out from your heart to the left and the right, far in each direction... ...

And feel a third stream of light from your heart streaming out to the front, and out into the back of your heart space, far out in front and way out behind you.

Feel your consciousness centred firmly within, in your heart, and able to flow out and back again at will in all directions along the streams of Light - north, east, south, west, below and above. This is your Star Cross.

You are experiencing yourself as a star now, centred in your heart and shining your Light out into far distances where your radiance can be seen far off in the cosmos...

Feel yourself in your Star Cross, and know that the Star Councils of Light see you shining the Love in your Hearts out into the cosmos so brightly...

And they see the whole Planet Earth lighting up as more and more of you take the time to centre yourselves in your hearts and begin to shine.

Now, breathe in your Love for all humankind into your hearts and as you breathe out, see your Love flowing out to enfold the place where you live, and all the people and animals, the birds and the trees, the grass and flowers that live around you.

Breathe in your Love for all humankind and all life upon this planet... And feel the Light of your Love flowing out in all four directions, spreading further to encompass the whole of the country you live in, all the towns and cities, the countryside and the rivers and forests, mountains and seas.

Now with the next inspiration breathe in your Love for the Earth under your feet, and on the out breath send the Light of your Love down the stream of light below, deep down into the Earth your Mother….

Take a few breaths to connect with the Earth right down into her core… sending her your love and your gratitude for sustaining your life through all the changes she has been going through…

And finally on your next inbreath breathe in your Love and focus upwards on the vertical stream of light of your Star Cross… and as you breathe out send the Light of your Love up from your heart through your head and out of your crown…

Send the Light of your Love up to your Star Brothers and Sisters of the Star Nations who are waiting close by to assist your planet…

They too need to feel the Love of your Hearts and your welcome, so you may work together for the wholesome future of your dear blue-green planet.

And feel their Love for you, dear Human Brothers and Sisters, take it into your Hearts, and receive their Blessings upon you…

Take a few moments to feel the Blessings of the Star Councils of Light settling softly upon you and filtering into your hearts...

And now, feeling the Blessings of the Star Councils of Light all around you and all through you, slowly draw in your light... draw in your consciousness, slowly back through the arms of your Star Cross... down from the vertical... up from the earth... and inwards from the four directions...

Slowly feel the Light of your Love concentrating within you, settling and centring in your heart... Come right back in now... and sense the boundaries of the bubble of your aura about 3-4 feet, about a metre, all around you. Feel yourself centred securely in your heart.

And rest in the Peace of your Heart, trusting that all will be done that the Power of Love and Light can bring about to help the evolution of the planet Earth, and all Life upon the Earth.

Know that the Star Councils of Light are with you always, and hold you in their Love.

Amuna Ra, for the Star Councils of Light,

April 2013

Integration,

Signatures

and

Star Being

Consciousness

MORE ON MAKING CIRCLES AND SIGNATURES

At the end of the 2012 crop circle season, I was in conversation with Peroptimé about the great formation at Hackpen Hill of 26 August. I found I was still processing the information that a higher part of my being was involved. The assimilation was to take all winter and spring, and I share part of my process here, trusting it will help others who are finding it is not always the easiest task to integrate their growing awareness of their Star Selves. For it requires a considerable stretching of the mind, and a huge expansion in our conception of what a human being is, of what we *all* are in our greater beings. It is also one thing to be inwardly aware of these truths, and another to speak openly of them in personal terms.

Many will regard all this with utter scepticism, especially if they do not yet have experience of the spiritual aspects of their own being, or if the concept of intergalactic star beings standing behind the ancient gods and angelic beings, and indeed behind our own Higher Selves, is just too far out. I would also have felt that not so very many years ago, but my experiences since have opened me to a great deal to which I was previously closed.

In seeking clarification, and to help me get used to what was being revealed, I would sometimes ask deliberately simple questions as in the following conversations. You will notice the star beings also reply to unvoiced thoughts.

Peroptimé, for the Star Councils of Light:

Yes, you know it was I who made this great one (*the formation at Hackpen Hill of 26 August 2012*) with the help of Metatron himself, for we did use his cube in its construction, we Andromedans of the Andromedan Fleet, captained by your beloved Wasaki-Quetzalcoatl.

Anaximander my brother, myself and my Lord Wasaki. We made it together from our small craft that flies from the mothership when you give the word from your console where you monitor the needs and the changes in the pulses of the land and its peoples.

Amuna Ra: When I make a circle like the two small ones at Hackpen Hill (*both reported on 21 August 2012, pp. 130 and 134*), do I fly down in a small craft? And how do I make them?

Peroptimé: You do use a small craft, dear one, and you use the laser power of light as we do to make the circles and set the energies. Sometimes you are accompanied by one of us, but if it is a Pleiadian circle, you set the energies and direct the beams of light.

You wonder if you made the Knoll Down formation of last year (p.14) that you were so happy in, and the simple circle at Cherhill this year. Of course you did, dearest sister, that is why you rejoiced to feel the strength of your own energy rising from the land. You were completely at home in the Pleiadian energies and loved to be in these circles which transported you into your simultaneous star being existence.

You need the re-charging of your own formations when you are working in your human body, go often when you have the chance, dearest one. Use the possibilities of these days, when they remain to be visited before the harvesting time.

Amuna Ra, Star Self: You wish to know of the two small circles outside the main circles at Cherhill (25 June 2012, p.63), this too is a signature, of the being you know as ...

Amuna Ra: Oh! I am feeling ... Amuna Ra, my Star Self... But what about the cross of the Hackpen Hill circle signature? (*21 August, p. 130*)

Amuna Ra, Star Self: It is you, dear one. Your signature is both two small circles, and the square cross signifying the Earth.

Amuna Ra: Why are there two signatures? That seems to be a contradiction in terms.

Amuna Ra, Star Self: That is only so in earthly terms. You give your earthly signature, the equal-armed cross, for a circle with earthly connotations, and your cosmic signature for circles of cosmic significance.

Amuna Ra: Did 'I' also make the other circles with double small circles?

Amuna Ra, Star Self: Oh yes, dear one, *we* made them all!

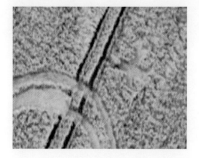 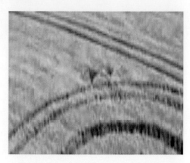

Earthly cross, Hackpen Hill - 21 August 12 *Small cosmic circles, Cherhill - 25 June 12*

Signatures of Peroptimé (Sandalphon) and Anaximander (Metatron)

These two signature glyphs appeared beside the Solstice Flower at Golden Ball Hill on 20 June 2012 (p. 54.) I add them here for reference.

 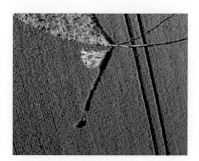

Wasaki-Quetzalcoatl, Commander of the Andromedan Fleet

Wasaki is the star being who first made contact with me in August 2009 on behalf of the Galactic Federation and called me to my work of channelling and being a bridge to the Star Councils of Light. He has been a close companion ever since in this extraordinary journey, and I am so pleased in my heart to be in frequent communication with him now.

Self Portrait with Peace Pipe, Cherhill - 27 July 2011   © *Steve Alexander*

Wasaki, best known as Quetzalcoatl, who was prophesied to return to the Earth at the end of the Mayan Calendar, coinciding with the Winter Solstice of the year of 2012. Many crop circle researchers recognised his portrayals in the crop circles of previous years that depicted huge Mayan headdresses and in the great serpents snaking through the fields. Quezalcoatl was known as having an element of the joker, and this is evident here at Cherhill. He told me this was his 'self portrait with peace pipe', but that he 'cannot really smoke' (!) though he does truly wish for peace amongst human beings, and with them. This crop circle remained for weeks in the field below the White Horse and obelisk at Cherhill, in line with the formation that bore his signature glyph at Jubilee Plantation, the grand finale of 2011.

Quetzalcoatl's signature at Jubilee Plantation, Cherhill - 15 Aug 2011, above and below beside the magnificent crop circle which was the 2011 finake   © Steve Alexander

Twelve years before his Self Portrait appeared in 2012, Quetzalcoatl's glyph appeared in this crop circle on 18 July 1999. It was also at Cherhill, in the very same field below the obelisk and the White Horse.

Cherhill – 18 July 1999   *© Steve Alexander*

Star Being Heads

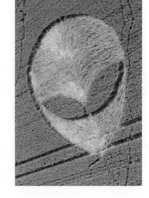

There have been several heads of star beings depicted in the crop circles in recent years, all very like the one here at Hinton Parva, on 25 July 2012. Charlbury Hill of 20 July 2011 was almost identical to this, and both are like Quetzalcoatl's self-portrait in proportion and in their dark eyes formed from standing crop.

© APS Ltd/WCCSG

Star Connecting

At the Solstice of 2009 this crop circle appeared below the White Horse at Alton Barnes. It had the same theme of rectangular transformers to transduce the frequency of the energy as the City of Light in 2012, which was in the field across the road. (pp. 69 and 84). Central is the still head of a star being with large eyes, softly indicated in the lay. Eight days later, on 29 June this star being head was repeated nearby at South Field, Alton Priors (p. 199) These heads are very like the one at Cherhill on 27 July 2011 (p. 192) which Wasaki claimed as his 'self-portrait'. All have the same geometrical proportions, and to me they clearly indicate their star being creators in the Star Councils of Light.

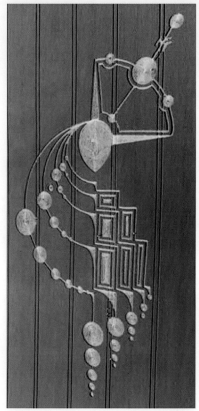

Alton Barnes White Horse – 21 June 2009
© *Steve Alexander*

Here, the astrolabe-like forms and the curving lines connecting to the circles leading to the transformers all project out from the star being's head, illustrating how their consciousness directs the flow of energy in both directions, between the earth and the mother ship, which constantly monitors the process of administering the doses of healing energy and adjusts the frequencies of the cosmic rays coded to balance the earth and awaken human beings. The long streams of codes were added eight days after the crop circle first appeared on 29 June 2009.

My Star Awakening

In the channelling that follows, Peroptimé speaks to show me how they were calling me to work with them weeks before I consciously knew of it, through the beautiful Swallow formation that graced the fields of Alton Barnes just after the Summer Solstice of 2009, and two day before the codes were added to the Solstice formation. This is of course only one interpretation of the Swallow crop circle, and a most personal story, told because it was me who enquired of the meaning as I was finishing this book. Had it been a mathematician who had asked, no doubt quite other layers of meaning would have been brought to the surface, for the crop circles speak in a star language more akin to the Quantum world of the new physics, a world which has multi-faceted possibilities of interpretation, where we each receive what is right in the moment, and what is in accord with our personal consciousness and connection to the star beings and spiritual worlds.

And this does not invalidate the general messages that the star beings transmit, for even with those intended for a great many people, individuals tell me again and again that they feel directly addressed and helped in their personal lives. This ability to speak to the individual consciousness of very many different people at once is a hallmark of high spiritual beings communicating through a clear channel. That said, I do think we need to use our discernment about all channelling that we come across, including that which is in this book, as to whether it resonates within our own heart as true. It is the heart that is the spiritual sense organ most appropriate for the perception of cosmic truths, even if our heads may find various aspects difficult to comprehend or to accept, we will sense what is true in our heart.

Opposite: Alton Barnes White Horse, phase 2 - 29 June 2009   © Steve Alexander

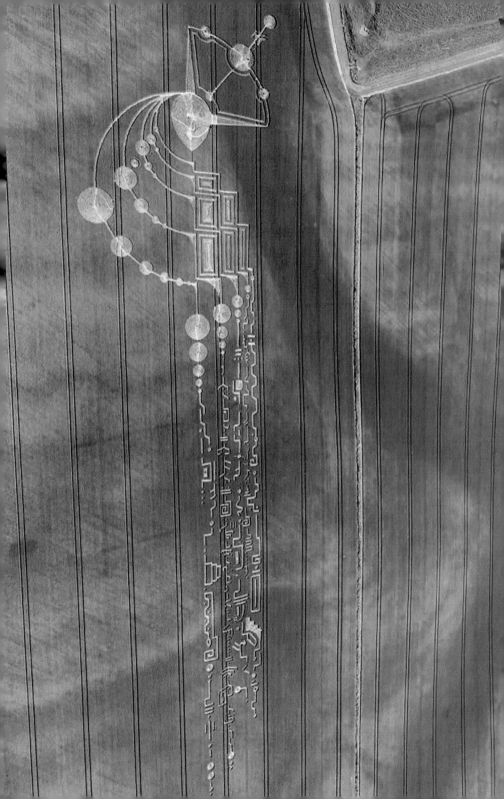

Awakening to Star Being Consciousness

Peroptimé, for the Star Councils of Light:

This graceful swallow we made to bring you joy, that you may soar to the heights of the cosmos. The swallow is our mothership overarching the earth, and embracing the earth. From the two smaller lightships flow streams of codes to activate the dormant strands of DNA within those human beings who are ready. And in the centre from our embrace of the earth the streams of codes continue and are received in the consciousness of our colleague who is working upon the earth.

She does not know yet that she is our colleague for the codes are only now beginning to stream into her consciousness. She is beginning to awaken and soon she will recognise she is a star being in her other self. The codes are being transmitted into her consciousness. They are starting to change her. She is freeing herself to take up our work very soon. Rapid will be the shifts in her consciousness. Her mind will expand dramatically and she will come into the circles in this season soon.

Yes, dearest Amuna Ra, this is a picture of our calling you to a consciousness of our work together, to awaken you to your Star Self's mission, and to your own star being. It is your friend and colleague, Peroptimé, who speaks with you now, and who is overjoyed that you are reaching a truly simultaneous consciousness of our mission upon the earth.

Peroptimé,

11 April 2013

Opposite: South Field, Alton Priors – 27 June 2009   *© Steve Alexander*

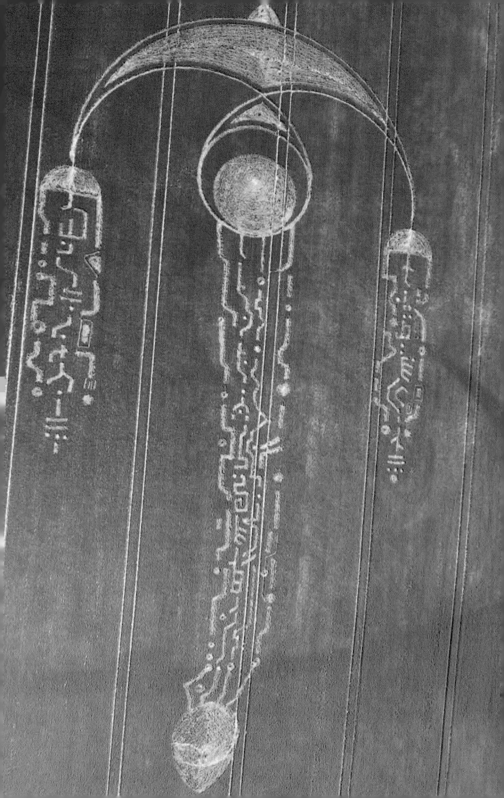

Post Script

Accepting my Star Counterpart

Peroptimé referred to the long stream of codes in the centre of the 2009 crop circle at South Field as being transmitted into *my* consciousness, and it is only now when I look once more at the photograph that I notice that the codes are streaming down into the *star being's* head. This did not seem to me at all unusual when I channelled the words in April 2013. So I see that by then I had inwardly accepted myself as a star being. The process of integrating this multi-dimensional consciousness is complete. I *know* now that I am a star being in a simultaneous existence, and that she is a higher aspect of my earthly consciousness.

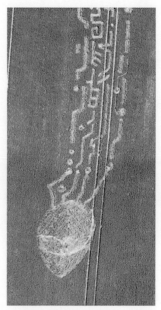

South Field - 27 June 2009
© Steve Alexander

More and more I find myself for a moment seeing through my Star Self's big dark blue eyes, eyes that have a much more all-round vision. At these times I am especially aware of her/my lightness of being and our joyous approach to life, full of love. We are distinct beings, yet we can merge when we wish. Hers is a vast consciousness, like a huge cosmic sphere all around, just waiting for the human me to focus more on exploring the inter-dimensional levels now opening to me.

It is complete, for I have stopped resisting - stopped being worried what people will think. I have allowed myself to experience my Star Self, my galactic counterpart, from within.

She is in me and I am in her. We are one.

Amuna Ra, Calne, Wiltshire, 21 June 2013

P.P.S.

A Photo of my Star Counterpart

To my astonishment a few weeks later I discovered a digital image of a blue star being's round head with large dark eyes and a purple blush to the skin like a damson – which is just like how I see my star counterpart. I felt a great shock of recognition, and could hardly believe what I saw on the website, but I knew in my heart it was her. The photo is on the BLT Research site, posted by Nancy Talbott, a long-standing crop circle researcher in America and a friend of the man who took the photograph. You can see it if you follow the link in the Endnotes[vi]. I am most grateful to her unstinting efforts to make his work known to English speakers.

The extraordinary photo was taken in a crop circle field in Holland on 15 September 2012 by Robbert van den Broeke, using the camera of a member of a Dutch film crew who were filming him at the time. Robbert is a very sensitive medium and healer who has the remarkable ability to take photographs of beings in the Fourth Dimension when he senses their presence. He has recorded many wonderful images of angels and star beings with an ordinary digital camera, and has a most interesting website for his work.[vii] I hope there will be the chance to meet him soon.

This is what my counterpart told me with great delight:

Amuna Ra – Star Counterpart:

It is so like you, because it *is* you, Amuna Ra! You are one of the star beings who work through him, as is Peroptimé-Sandalphon. It is I, Amuna Ra, who speaks - I who am now also within you as your Higher Self, your constant connection to your Star Self, the Pleiadian body which you inhabit when you work aboard the City of Light, and which our dear Robbert has photographed.

Amuna Ra, 19 July 2013

I look forward to the story unfolding...

ACKNOWLEDGEMENTS

There are many people - and beings - I would like to thank for their help and support in the process of writing and publishing this book:

The Star Councils of Light

Firstly, my deep gratitude to my friends and colleagues in the Star Councils of Light, without whom there would have been no book and likely no crop circles, and whose ever present love, humour and words of wisdom have helped me survive extraordinary learning curves with computers and my first venture into the world of publishing.

Photographers

I would also like to express my great gratitude to the photographers whose beautiful images grace these pages and make visual sense of my words and of those of the Star Councils of Light:

- To Steve Alexander - whose exquisite aerial photos form the major part of the crop circle illustrations. And I much appreciated the stimulating conversations in crop circles with Steve and Karen.
  www.temporarytemples.co.uk
- To Philippe Ullens of the Henge Shop, Avebury, for his generosity in contributing his photos to this book, especially for the beautifully atmospheric cover image of Avebury and the Family of Dragons.
  www.hengeshop.com
- To Clare Oatley of the Wiltshire Crop Circle Study Group for sourcing various of their lovely photos for me.
  www.wccsg.co.uk

- To Monique Klinkenbergh, for the photograph only she had taken.
  www.cropcircleaccess.com
- To Lucy Pringle, for supplying the image that was missing.
  www.lucypringle.co.uk
- To Mark Fussell of Crop Circle Connector for letting me use two of their images to complete the set.
  www.cropcircleconnector.co.uk
- And lastly, I thank all the photographers who have made available in the public domain their images that I have used to illustrate earthly and astronomical reflections of the teachings of the Star Councils of Light.

Friends and Family

Amongst the many friends, workshop participants and people all over the world who cherish the words of the Star Councils of Light and who have held me in their thoughts during the preparation of this book, there are four to whom I would specially like to express my heartfelt gratitude:

- Christina Sieber, for her dedicated reading through of the manuscripts, helpful suggestions, and support in ensuring I acquired all the images I needed.
- John Salter, for his faith in my work, sanctuary when needed, and support in the publishing stages.
- Miriam Rose, who gave me invaluable warmth and help in the bizarre circumstances of the final stages.
- Monica Bailey, whose instant understanding and will to help was balm to my soul.

And finally I would like to thank my children and theirs - my three lovely grand-daughters - who all saw precious little of me while I was immersed in the book. I look forward to spending much more time with you all now!

RESOURCES

BOOKS

Here is a selection of books that I have enjoyed - about Avebury and about the crop circles by long-standing researchers. There are very many more available.

An Introduction to Crop Circles, Andy Thomas, Wessex Books, 2011. An easily accessible introduction to the range of the phenomenon, including the star being faces at Chilbolton, 2001, and Crabwood, 2002.

Avebury Cosmos, Nicholas R. Mann, O Books, 2011. An interesting and erudite book on the ancient astronomical alignments of the Avebury Henge.

Avebury, Sun Moon and Earth, Maria Wheatley and Busty Taylor, Wessex Bools, 2011. A good quick-reference guide to the sacred landscape of Avebury, which gives seasonal alignments with the stones.

Crop Circles, the Bones of God, Michael Glickman, Frog Books, 2009. A beautifully written and illustrated memoir with lots on the geometry and design of the formations, which ends on a presentiment of imminent extra-terrestrial contact, which could have been the forward to this book.

Crop Circles, the Evidence, Janet Ossebard, Benign Publishers, 2009. This is part of an excellent series of eight books. Here she presents a lively wide-ranging approach to proving that the majority of the crop circles are not man-made, with many eye witness accounts and personal experiences.

Crop Circles, the Greatest Mystery of Modern Times, Lucy Pringle, Thorsons, 1999. An extensive review of the earlier period up to 1998, including the author's research into the scientific effects on animals and people.

Messages from Space: Crop Circles bring the First Indisputable Extraterrestrial Signs from Space, Jay Goldner, Michael Wiese Productions, 2002. Beautifully illustrated and researched, this book is centred on the extraterrestrial communications in the formations which appeared next to the Chilbolton Observatory in 2001.

Quest for Contact, a True Story of Crop Circles, Psychics and UFOs, Andy Thomas & Paul Bura, SB Publications, 1997. A lively account of early researchers and psychic experiments.

Sophia's Egg, Bert Janssen, Frontier Publishing, 2011. A novel about contemporary spiritualty and intrigues in the crop circle world, set in the Wiltshire Downs around Avebury. I found some strong hints within for which I am grateful.

The Crop Circle Year Books, Steve and Karen Alexander, Temporary Temples Press. Full of Steve's lovely aerial photographs and Karen's beautiful coloured drawings and sensitive commentaries.

The Hypnotic Power of Crop Circles, Bert Janssen, Frontier Publishing, 2004. Emphasis on the geometry, including step by step exercises on constructing the designs, and leading to the conclusion that it is a higher aspect of ourselves which makes the circles – which dovetails with my journey in this book, though reached by a quite different route.

WORKSHOPS & COURSES with AMUNA RA

Star Connecting Courses, Star Journey Weekends and Crop Circle Workshops – along with other themes – can be found on my websites:

www. AmunaRa.com   &   www. PleiadianRegression.co.uk

CONTACT

Amuna@AmunaRa.com   or   Amuna@PleiadianRegression.co.uk

ENDNOTES

i   **Sandalphon**   (Hebrew: סָנְדַּלְפוֹן;   Greek: Σανδαλφών)   is
an **archangel** in **Jewish** and **Christian** writings.   Sandalphon   figures
prominently in the mystical literary traditions of **Rabbinic Judaism** and
early **Christianity**, notably in the **Midrash**, **Talmud**, and **Kabbalah**.

Some of the earliest sources on Sandalphon refer to him as
the **prophet Elijah** transfigured and elevated to **angelic** status.[1] Other
sources (mainly from the **midrashic** period) describe him as the "twin
brother" of **Metatron**, whose human origin as **Enoch** was similar to the
human origin of Sandalphon.[2]

http://en.wikipedia.org/wiki/Sandalphon

ii In the Avebury area each season there are several crop formations
made by various groups of human beings, some by skilled artists on the
ground, others by utilising advanced computer, GPS and technological
skills; some are made by amateurs and others professionally
commissioned with the consent of the farmer, for example the proposal
of marriage to Laura at Uffcott on 3 September 2012.

The Star Councils of Light expressly wanted me to point out which crop
circles they did not make in 2012, and I have listed these below.

AVEBURY CROP CIRCLES OF 2012
NOT MADE BY THE STAR COUNCILS OF LIGHT:

1. Boreham Woods, Lockeridge – 5 July 2012
2. Juggler's Lane, Yatesbury - 17 July 2012
3. Allington, Devizes - 24 July 2012
4. Hill Barn, East Kennett - 26 July 2012
5. Devil's Den, Fyfield - 12 August 2012
6. Lurkeley Hill, East Kennett - 19 August 2012

7. Uffcott, Broad Hinton - 3 September 2012
8. The Ridgeway, near Overton Hill - 5 September 2012

[iii] *www.cropcircleconnector.com* is a useful resource. They record the crop circles as they are reported, with map references, and have pages for comments.

[iv] 'One of Wheatstone's most ingenious devices was the 'Polar Clock,' exhibited at the meeting of the British Association in 1848. It is based on the fact discovered by Sir David Brewster, that the light of the sky is polarised in a plane at an angle of ninety degrees from the position of the sun. It follows that by discovering that plane of polarisation, and measuring its azimuth with respect to the north, the position of the sun, although beneath the horizon, could be determined, and the apparent solar time obtained. The clock consisted of a spyglass, having a nicol (double-image) prism for an eyepiece, and a thin plate of selenite for an object-glass. When the tube was directed to the North Pole—that is, parallel to the Earth's axis—and the prism of the eyepiece turned until no colour was seen, the angle of turning, as shown by an index moving with the prism over a graduated limb, gave the hour of day. The device is of little service in a country where watches are reliable; but it formed part of the equipment of the 1875-1876 North Polar Expedition...' (http://en.wikipedia.org/wiki/Charles_Wheatstone)

[v] http://www.davideicke.com David Eicke has worked tirelessly for decades to awaken people to the forces behind the scenes since his own awakening to higher consciousness, and his meditation dovetailed with what the Star Councils of Light sent through me.

[vi] http://www.bltresearch.com/robbert.php

[vii] http://www.robbertvandenbroeke.com